NAPA VALLEY
ENTERTAINING

BLAKESLEY CHAPPELLET
Photography by Briana Marie

Historic Hospitality Books

Table of Contents

With Gratitude

To the hosts who were courageous enough to open their homes and wineries and share the stories, recipes, and style that brings *Napa Valley Entertaining* to life on these pages: I am inspired by each of you and beyond proud to share your creativity and passion.

To Margarita for teaching me to be brave and aim high, to persevere and always give my all.

To Molly for being a remarkable role model in entertaining and in life.

To Deirdre, Kerry, Karen, Linda, and Lisa for their encouragement to embark on this endeavor.

To Briana for her extraordinary eye, artistry, photographic talent, and incredible spirit: I am truly grateful you joined me on this project. My thanks extend to your fabulous assistants, Brian, Cecilia, Anna, Brandon, and Trevor.

To Chris, Sheila, Vicky, Betsy, Kristin, Wanda, Julia, Linda, and everyone at Historic Hospitality Books: you have been a dream team to work with. My thanks for your patience in guiding me on my maiden journey in publishing.

To Cyril for his support, patience, humor, and love.

Introduction

A patchwork of vineyards, charming towns, world-class wineries, and celebrated restaurants, Napa Valley has entertaining at its very heart. To me, it is the people of the valley that bring this place to life. The incredibly diverse population that calls Napa Valley home have come for a shared reason: our passion for wine and connection to the land. Gathering to share food and conversation over a glass of wine brings us joy.

Napa Valley Entertaining provides an entrée into the lives of a handful of the valley's celebrated hosts—both newcomers and second- and third-generation vintners. In these pages, we will step into a theater of the senses during dinner with Jean-Charles Boisset, sit on the vineyard deck for a colorful supper with designer Barbara Colvin, enjoy a bit of Latino culture over ceviche and chardonnay at a fiesta with the Ceja family, partake in an indulgent lobster feed with St. Helena's fire chief, go hog wild at a barbecue with the Baggetts, and sing around the firepit with Silver Oak's David Duncan. In their personal entertaining, the hosts give insight on their passion for food, wine, and flair, sharing their favorite recipes, tips on throwing a party, and stories of how they came to the valley. As different as they are, the hosts are bound by one common thread: their desire to create a unique and memorable experience for their guests.

I was introduced to Napa in a unique way—not as a tourist but as an insider. Nearly two decades ago, I married a second-generation vintner and moved to Napa Valley. I immediately became one of the valley's hosts, opening our home to VIPs and customers. My husband, Cyril, and I have had the great pleasure of entertaining CEOs, Academy Award–winning actors, Grammy-winning musicians, and hundreds of other lovely people on Pritchard Hill. Stepping into this role was intimidating at first. What do you serve Mr. Grammy winner for lunch? Over the years, however, I've realized that the essence of entertaining is being authentic. Our guests are looking for an experience that is real, passionate, and genuine. They want to create their own story and connection to a bottle of Chappellet wine. Our lives have been greatly enriched by spending time with so many interesting and diverse individuals.

I know you will be inspired, as I have been, by the breathtaking settings, beautiful tables, stunning florals, sumptuous food, and wonderful details these hosts have created. When dining at a friend's home, I love to discover new ideas for my own entertaining. My hope is that these pages will provide you with fresh ideas for a party or a meal and allow you to bring more than a glass of Napa Valley wine to your own table.

—BLAKESLEY CHAPPELLET

A Victorian Valentine

To enter the Ackerman Heritage House is to step back in time to the elegance of the 1880s. This Queen Anne Victorian, located just two blocks from Napa's Main Street, was built in 1889 and painstakingly restored over five years by owner Lauren Ackerman. Striving to show the old house in its glory days, Lauren filled it with period-correct antique furnishings and created a true living museum. "I wanted something to help us remember the past because it helps shape our future," she says. The love and care she took in restoring this grand piece of Napa's history is a gift to the city and the community.

Entertaining at the Ackerman Heritage House is always a history lesson for Lauren, who studied the Victorian era extensively while restoring the building. She works to make every event authentic to the era and season, from the food and drink to the décor and music. While the inspiration for most meals comes from a collection of cookbooks from the 1800s, she works to put a modern spin on the recipes.

On the eve of Valentine's Day, Lauren invited some of her favorite couples over for a meal fit for Queen Victoria, including a decadent chocolate dessert. A collection of valentines from the Victorian era covered the receiving room table, where guests could explore the intricate pop-up, multidimensional cards. Simple, authentic love notes from the period were placed at each setting in the formal dining room. The tablescape also featured vintage heart-shaped gift boxes, an arrangement of red roses in a stunning silver tureen, and a towering candelabra.

"It's a good thing that wine is timeless," says Lauren, who always serves cabernet from her Coombsville estate. "In fact, the history of the home and grape farming in Napa Valley run parallel, since the first vineyards were planted in the area in the mid-1800s." That evening, her guests raised a glass to toast Lauren's vision and generosity—grateful to be surrounded by the love and passion she put into every inch of the historic mansion.

Below: Built in 1889, Ackerman Heritage House is on Napa's National Register of Historic Places. Visitors are welcome to taste Ackerman's wines in the Aviary Carriage House by appointment. Opposite: The formal dining room was set for a Valentine's eve celebration.

Right: Each guest received a vintage love note. Below: Cookbooks from the 1800s inspired the meal. Opposite, clockwise from top: Lauren displayed a collection of valentines from the turn of the century. Ackerman's Cabernet Sauvignon paired beautifully with the cake.

Lauren Ackerman

Lauren's career has taken her from working with entrepreneurial technology businesses, to founding her own firm to help Fortune 500 companies set up distribution channels in technology, to creating a winery known for its artisan cabernet sauvignon. Lauren and her husband, Bob, established Ackerman Family Vineyards after moving to Napa in 1994. Passionate about the arts and education, Lauren serves on a number of nonprofit boards, including di Rosa Preserve.

Raspberry Cabernet Cake

Makes 12 servings

2½ cups cake flour or all-purpose flour	2½ cups sugar, divided
¾ cup dark or natural unsweetened cocoa powder	¾ cup unsalted butter, melted
1 teaspoon baking powder	¼ cup vegetable oil
¼ teaspoon salt	5 large eggs
1 cup cabernet sauvignon or other red wine	1 tablespoon vanilla extract
¼ cup light sour cream	1 tablespoon chocolate extract or additional vanilla extract
12 ounces fresh raspberries	Chocolate Red Wine Glaze
	Powdered sugar

Preheat oven to 350 degrees. Grease a 12-cup bundt pan and dust with cocoa powder.

Sift flour and cocoa powder into a medium bowl. Stir in baking powder and salt. Combine wine and sour cream in a small bowl and mix well.

Set aside a few raspberries for garnish, if desired. Combine remaining raspberries and ¼ cup sugar in a small bowl and stir gently.

Combine butter, vegetable oil, and remaining 2¼ cups sugar in a mixing bowl. Beat at medium speed with an electric mixer for 3 minutes or until light and well blended. Add eggs, one at a time, beating just until blended after each addition. Stir in vanilla and chocolate extract. Add flour mixture alternately with wine mixture, beating at low speed just until blended after each addition. Fold in raspberry mixture. Pour batter into prepared pan.

Bake for 50 to 55 minutes or until a long skewer inserted into center of cake comes out clean. Cool cake in pan on a wire rack for 30 minutes. Invert onto a wire rack placed over a rimmed baking sheet. Let stand to cool completely.

Drizzle Chocolate Red Wine Glaze over cake, spooning glaze from baking sheet back over top of cake. Sift powdered sugar over cake. Garnish with reserved raspberries.

CHOCOLATE RED WINE GLAZE

2 tablespoons butter	1 cup sifted powdered sugar
2 tablespoons dark or natural unsweetened cocoa powder	1 teaspoon vanilla extract
¼ cup heavy whipping cream	2 tablespoons cabernet sauvignon or other red wine

Melt butter in a small saucepan over medium-low heat. Whisk in cocoa powder and cream. Cook for 2 minutes, whisking constantly. Remove from heat and stir in powdered sugar. Add vanilla and wine, whisking until smooth (glaze will thicken as it cools). Makes 1 cup.

Menu

Celery Root Soup
Basil and Lobster
Lloyd Cellars Chardonnay

Sautéed Diver Scallops
and Foie Gras
Ackerman Alavigna Tosca

Akaushi Beef Striploin
Mushrooms, Kale,
Potatoes, Bordelaise
Ackerman Cabernet Sauvignon

Raspberry Cabernet Cake
Raspberries, Cream
Library Cabernet Sauvignon

Hollywood Meets Vine

Opposite: Brass scales and pops of lavender and crimson colors added dramatic flare to a sophisticated table. Below: When Rich Frank purchased this 1930s Tudor home, he wasn't aware of the exceptional grape quality in the surrounding vineyard. His and Leslie's Calistoga winery was voted "Best Napa Winery" by the Bay Area A-List for many years. It welcomes guests daily. Appointments are recommended.

Frank Family Vineyards is one of the few estates in Napa Valley to produce both still and sparkling wine. Their stone winery is the third oldest in Napa, with roots that date back to 1884, and is recognized on the National Register of Historic Places. Visitors are welcomed like members of the family to sample wines at the winery's tasting room, located in a restored yellow Craftsman house.

Gathering for dinner al fresco one harvest evening, guests joined proprietors Rich and Leslie Frank at their home in Rutherford. The house overlooks Winston Hill Vineyard, named for the Franks' late springer spaniel. There, Leslie created an outdoor lounge where guests enjoyed bubbles and hors d'oeuvres. Local Chef Nash Cognetti of Tre Posti started the evening by demonstrating how to make his famous Fresh Mozzarella, while Leslie wowed guests by opening a bottle of Frank Family sparkling wine with a saber. She explains, "In 1958, our winery was home to Hanns Kornell Champagne Cellars, so making sparkling wine has been in our DNA since our founding in 1992."

Leslie's table made a sophisticated statement on the front lawn. Lavender-colored water goblets and patterned Versace plates on gold chargers complemented cabernet-colored florals in an eclectic assortment of vases. Massive brass scales held the first course: platters of antipasti, paired with Frank Family's Carneros Chardonnay. The Mediterranean-inspired dinner also featured fresh tomatoes from Rich and Leslie's vegetable garden.

The Franks, who had careers in television, find parallels between producing TV programs and creating wine. "You can't make good wine without good grapes, and you can't make good TV shows or movies without a good script," says Rich. "You need a winemaker who controls the process; in the movie business, the director has that role."

The spectacular setting and delicious meal were enhanced by the Franks' warmth and engaging conversation. Looking out at the vine covered landscape while sipping the Frank's wines, guests gained a newfound appreciation for the hard work and teamwork involved in winemaking.

Clockwise from right: Brass candlesticks and intricate Versace plates added a touch of formality to the dining table. Leslie shared Frank Family's Brut Rosé with guests prior to dinner. An antipasto course was set on brass scales and in an assortment of small bowls.

Rich and Leslie Frank

Rich's love for wine came from his international travels as the president of Disney Studios. He founded Frank Family Vineyards in 1992, when he purchased the winery in Calistoga. Prior to his tenure at Disney Studios, Rich was president of the Paramount Television Group and is currently vice chairman of the American Film Institute. Leslie, an Emmy award–winning journalist, spent more than twenty-five years as a news anchor and reporter, the last decade of which was spent at KABC in Los Angeles. The Franks adopted their German shepherd, Riley, in 2010.

"We love to share the beauty of our surroundings and the fruits of our labor with the people close to us. Exuding a warm atmosphere at dinner with good wine and food, paired with lively and meaningful conversation, are the moments we cherish the most." —LESLIE FRANK

Basil Tagliatelle with Tomato Fig Sugo

Makes 4 to 6 servings

Basil Tagliatelle	6 Black Mission figs, stemmed and halved
Tomato Fig Sugo	1 tablespoon honey
4 slices guanciale, pancetta, or prosciutto, cut into 1-inch-wide strips	⅔ cup freshly grated Pecorino Romano cheese
1 tablespoon extra-virgin olive oil	

Prepare Basil Tagliatelle up to a day ahead. Prepare Tomato Fig Sugo and keep warm. Meanwhile, preheat oven to 325 degrees.

Wrap guanciale around cannoli molds (you can also wrap bundles of bamboo skewers with foil to create cylinders). Place on a parchment-lined baking sheet. Bake for 10 minutes or until golden brown. Cool slightly and slide twists off molds onto paper towels. Cool completely.

Heat a cast-iron or heavy skillet over high heat until very hot. Add olive oil and figs, cut sides down, and cook for 10 to 30 seconds or until lightly charred on the edges. Transfer figs, cut sides up, to a plate and brush with honey. Keep warm.

Bring an extra-large pot of salted water to a boil over medium-high heat. Cook Basil Tagliatelle for 1 to 3 minutes or just until al dente; drain. Divide Tomato Fig Sugo among 4 to 6 heated bowls. Top with glazed figs, Pecorino Romano cheese, and guanciale fusilloni.

BASIL TAGLIATELLE

2 cups tightly packed basil leaves	4 cups all-purpose flour
5 large eggs	Semolina or all-purpose flour
1 teaspoon kosher salt	

Blanch basil in boiling salted water in a saucepan for 10 to 15 seconds. Plunge basil immediately into ice water to stop the cooking process. Drain well and squeeze leaves dry with paper towels. Chop the basil finely in a food processor by pulsing 4 or 5 times. Transfer to a bowl. Combine eggs and salt in a food processor; pulse several times until eggs are light and foamy. Add basil and pulse to combine. Add flour gradually, pulsing until a shaggy dough is formed.

Knead dough on a lightly floured surface for 8 minutes or until smooth. Wrap in plastic wrap and let rest for 15 minutes. Cut dough into thirds. Roll each portion into thin sheets with a pasta machine according to manufacturer's directions. Cut sheets into 2 (12-inch-long) sections. Cut each section into strips using a ¼-inch-wide cutting attachment and toss lightly in semolina or all-purpose flour to form a nest. (Pasta may be prepared a day ahead. Place nests on a baking sheet. Cover with kitchen towels and place in the refrigerator.) Makes 6 nests.

TOMATO FIG SUGO

3 pounds ripe tomatoes	Kosher salt to taste
1 pound ripe Black Mission figs, stemmed and halved	2 garlic cloves, minced
	1 tablespoon chopped fresh oregano
½ cup plus 2 tablespoons extra-virgin olive oil, divided	4–5 fresh basil leaves
	Crushed red pepper flakes to taste

Core tomatoes and cut an X in each base. Blanch tomatoes in boiling water in a saucepan for 30 seconds and plunge into ice water to stop the cooking process. Peel tomatoes and cut crosswise into halves. Squeeze tomatoes, discarding seeds and liquid. Set aside.

Preheat oven to 500 degrees. Toss figs in 2 tablespoons olive oil. Place on a baking sheet and sprinkle with salt. Bake for 10 minutes. Set aside.

Heat remaining ½ cup olive oil in a saucepan over medium-low heat. Add garlic and cook until light golden brown, stirring occasionally. Stir in reserved tomatoes, reserved figs, oregano, and basil. Season well with salt and red pepper flakes. Bring mixture to a boil. Reduce heat and simmer for 1 hour. Purée with an immersion blender or process in a food mill and return to saucepan. Cook for 30 minutes or until thickened. Makes 4 cups.

Fresh Mozzarella

Makes 6 to 8 ounces

When making fresh mozzarella, the water must be uncomfortably hot. Use thin latex gloves, if desired, but do not allow water to seep into gloves. Serve and eat cheese immediately. Refrigeration makes it tough and rubbery.

6–8	ounces whole milk mozzarella curds
1	cup kosher salt
1	gallon water
	Toasted or grilled crostini
	Napa Valley olive oil
	Sea salt and freshly ground black pepper to taste

Break mozzarella curds into 1-inch pieces and place in a large stainless steel bowl. Let stand until room temperature. Combine several cups of ice and water in a medium bowl.

Combine salt and 1 gallon water in a large pot; bring to a boil. Reduce heat and simmer. Ladle small amounts of hot water down the sides of the stainless steel bowl. Let stand until curds melt, draining and adding more water if the water cools.

Push curds together to form one mass. Fold cheese over on top of itself repeatedly to form a ball, keeping it under hot water as much as possible, replacing water as it cools and dipping hands in ice water periodically to cool (water will be very hot).

Form a circle with forefinger and thumb of one hand. Push cheese through circle and gradually expand ring to allow cheese ball to fit through. Repeat several times until cheese is smooth and very elastic. Place cheese ball in cold water for 30 seconds to set shape.

Serve on toasted or grilled crostini, drizzled with olive oil. Sprinkle with sea salt and ground pepper.

Pan-Roasted Squab with Porcini Butternut Millefoglie and Vin Cotto

Makes 4 servings

1 cup kosher salt
¼ cup sugar
2 tablespoons orange zest
6 sprigs of fresh thyme
4 bone-in squab or Cornish game hen legs
2–3 cups duck fat
2 garlic cloves, minced
1 tablespoon butter

1 tablespoon olive oil
4 boneless, skin-on squab or Cornish game hen breasts
Salt and freshly ground black pepper to taste
Porcini Butternut Millefoglie
Vin Cotto

Combine kosher salt, sugar, orange zest, and thyme in a small bowl. Rub mixture evenly over squab legs and place in a glass baking dish. Cover legs with remaining salt mixture. Refrigerate, covered, for 2 hours.

Preheat oven to 275 degrees. Remove legs from curing mixture and rinse under cold water. Pat dry with paper towels and place in a baking dish just large enough to hold legs. Heat duck fat in a small saucepan just until melted; stir in garlic. Pour over squab legs. Bake, tightly covered, for 45 to 60 minutes or until tender. Cool squab legs in fat.

Heat butter and olive oil in a skillet over medium-low heat. Sprinkle squab breasts with salt and pepper and arrange, skin side down, in a skillet. Cook for 7 to 9 minutes or until golden brown, tilting pan and spooning butter mixture over squab. Turn breasts over and cook for 5 to 10 minutes or until a meat thermometer inserted into thickest portion registers 125 degrees for medium-rare (if using hens, cook to 165 degrees). Transfer to a platter; cover with foil and let rest for 5 minutes before slicing.

Place 1 Porcini Butternut Millefoglie in center of each plate. Arrange 1 leg confit towards back and fan slices of 1 squab breast toward front of each plate. Drizzle with ¼ cup Vin Cotto.

PORCINI BUTTERNUT MILLEFOGLIE

1 pound fresh porcini or large button mushrooms
1 small butternut squash
2 tablespoons butter

3 tablespoons chopped fresh sage
4 teaspoons light brown sugar
Salt and freshly ground black pepper to taste

Preheat oven to 375 degrees. Slice mushrooms thinly crosswise using a mandolin or sharp knife; set aside. Cut squash in half crosswise just to where the squash becomes bulbous and hollow with seeds. Peel the solid section and slice thinly using a mandolin at same setting as for mushrooms or a sharp knife. Line a baking sheet with parchment paper. Arrange mushrooms and squash in 4 spiraled circles, alternating mushrooms and squash and overlapping slices.

Heat butter in a small pan over medium heat. Cook for 1 minute or until golden brown. Remove from heat and stir in sage and brown sugar. Spoon butter mixture evenly over each circle and sprinkle with salt and pepper. Bake for 15 to 18 minutes or until squash is tender and edges turn golden brown. Cover and keep warm. Makes 4 servings.

VIN COTTO

1 pound cabernet grapes, stemmed, or fresh blackberries
3 cups cabernet sauvignon

1 teaspoon unsalted butter
Salt and freshly ground black pepper to taste

Place grapes in a non-aluminum saucepan over medium-high heat. Cook until skins burst and mixture becomes juicy, stirring constantly. Simmer over low heat for 25 to 30 minutes or until mixture is thick.

Stir in wine. Bring mixture to a boil. Simmer over low heat for 30 minutes or until thickened. Strain through a fine mesh strainer. Add butter, stirring until smooth. Stir in salt and pepper. Makes 1 cup.

Menu

Fresh Mozzarella "à la minute"
Brut Rosé

Antipasti Misti "Edible Table"
Carneros Chardonnay

Basil Tagliatelle
Carneros Pinot Noir

Pan-Roasted Squab
Winston Hill Cabernet Sauvignon

Baked Quince and Apple Gallette
and vanilla caramel

Opposite: Gorgeous floral arrangements play on the color of cabernet. The Franks' highly regarded

Winston Hill Red Wine is the flagship wine. Above: Chef Nash Cognetti of Tre Posti used garlic

blossoms, cabernet purée, and a sprig of fresh thyme to accent the squab.

A Gem of a Gelato Social

Crossing a stone footbridge to a tranquil oasis nestled under the oaks, guests leave the bustle of Napa Valley to enter Gemstone Vineyard, located in the heart of Yountville. The sixteen-acre estate is truly a jewel.

On a spectacular afternoon in July, families gathered at Gemstone for a grown-up take on an ice cream social. Hosted by proprietress Amy Marks Dornbusch and her husband, Adam, the event took place in a bohemian chic outdoor sanctuary. "I brought the indoors outside," says Amy, "moving chairs, lots of pillows and cushions, and even a couple of rugs from the tasting lounge into the garden." She added bouquets of succulents, eclectic metal and wood objects, and even a whimsical life-sized pig table for an infused-water station.

To make the casual gathering interactive and fun, Amy arranged a number of activities, setting up a bocce court in front of the barn and vintage board games, like Chinese checkers and Tiddlywinks, nearby. While some guests played games, others picked lemons and apple pears in the orchard. She then taught them how to craft a Furoshiki sack to carry their fruit or wine home.

On the menu were small bites. Amy's Gougères with Gruyère and Cherry Mostarda made it easy for the adults to play bocce and sip cabernet, while the kids ate Mt. Tam Tea Sandwiches and sipped water infused with raspberry, blackberry, and basil.

Gallons of homemade Lemon Olive Oil Gelato and Cabernet Granita were delivered in a gigantic block of ice in the back of Gemstone's vintage 1949 Dodge pickup truck. Flowers and grasses were frozen in the ice. To add a touch of flair, Amy set out Candied Lemon Slices and blocks of sea salt to grate over the gelato. She also hung rolls of tear-off MYdrap napkins from a manzanita branch.

Mother Nature plays a hand in the making of a gemstone, and she made her presence known with a breathtaking sunset over the Mayacamas. Gelato may have been central to Amy and Adam's summer gathering, but the real joy was bringing families together for a relaxing day in the country.

Below: Gemstone's modernized barn, with views of the vineyard, houses a chic tasting lounge for private guests. The vineyard is family-owned and operated, and there's no sign on the road. Opposite: A vintage pickup truck, adorned with olive branches and lavender, provided the perfect setting for serving gelato and granita.

Amy Marks Dornbusch

A California native, Amy Marks Dornbusch's passion for cooking and entertaining spurred her to found a catering and events company while living in Brooklyn, New York. Her love for a digital media executive brought her back to the Bay Area, where she married her husband, Adam, and joined her family's wine business. Now at the helm of Gemstone Vineyard, Amy is able to hone her business and creative talents, as well as nurture her love for gathering people over an inspired meal paired with exceptional wines.

"Entertaining is about making a huge impact with a small amount of effort. Re-think what you already have—utilize your garden for décor and ingredients, bring your furniture outdoors, and turn parting gifts into a fun activity for your guests." —AMY MARKS DORNBUSCH

Below: Amy's mother and best friend, Carole, inspired her to be innovative and fearless in entertaining, business, and life. Right: Gold and wooden objects and unusual floral arrangements adorned the table. Bottom: Guests could visit or play vintage games while sipping a glass of Gemstone in the makeshift outdoor lounge.

Gougères with Gruyère and Cherry Mostarda

Makes 2 dozen

½ cup water
½ cup whole milk
6 tablespoons butter, cubed
½ teaspoon salt
¼ teaspoon coarsely ground black pepper
⅛ teaspoon ground red pepper
1 cup all-purpose flour
4 large eggs

1½ cups (6 ounces) coarsely grated Gruyère cheese, divided
¼ cup minced fresh chives
8 ounces Gruyère cheese, sliced and cut into 24 (⅛-inch-thick) squares
Cherry Mostarda
Microgreens

Preheat oven to 425 degrees. Line two baking sheets with silicone baking mats or parchment paper.

Combine water, milk, butter, salt, black pepper, and red pepper in a small saucepan over medium-high heat; bring to a boil. Reduce heat to medium; add flour all at once and stir vigorously until mixture forms a ball that pulls away from sides of pan. Remove from heat and cool slightly. Transfer to a bowl. Add eggs, one at a time, stirring vigorously. Stir in 1 cup grated cheese and chives.

Spoon mixture into a pastry bag fitted with a large plain tip. Pipe mixture onto prepared baking sheets in small circular mounds about 2 inches wide and 1 inch apart and pat with wet fingertips to smooth the tops. (You may also drop mixture in heaping tablespoons onto prepared baking sheets.) Sprinkle with remaining ½ cup grated cheese. Bake for 10 minutes. Reduce oven temperature to 350 degrees and bake for 15 to 20 minutes or until golden brown, rotating pans, if necessary. Cool on wire racks. Slice each and fill with a slice of cheese, Cherry Mostarda, and microgreens.

CHERRY MOSTARDA

1 tablespoon mustard seeds
1 teaspoon whole pink peppercorns
½ teaspoon whole allspice
1 teaspoon coarse or flaked sea salt
¾ cup sugar
½ cup red wine

2 tablespoons red wine vinegar
1 tablespoon dry mustard
1 tablespoon Dijon mustard
2 cups fresh Bing cherries, stemmed and pitted, or frozen cherries, thawed

Grind mustard seeds, peppercorns, allspice, and salt coarsely with mortar and pestle. Mix spices, sugar, wine, vinegar, dry mustard, and Dijon mustard in a small saucepan over medium-high heat. Stir in cherries. Bring to a boil; reduce heat to medium. Cook for 25 minutes or until cherries are tender and mixture thickens, stirring frequently. Cool completely. Makes 1½ cups.

Note: May substitute 2 teaspoons ground mustard, 1¼ teaspoons coarse ground pepper, and ½ teaspoon ground allspice for the mustard seeds, peppercorns, and whole allspice.

Above: Fabric squares cut from remnants and vintage scissors were set out so guests could create Japanese Furoshiki carriers. Right: Gemstone's 1949 Dodge pickup truck. Opposite: Cherry Mostarda and microgreens added flavor and color to Gougères with Gruyère for a fresh take on tea sandwiches.

Menu

Gougères with Gruyère and Cherry Mostarda
Mt. Tam Tea Sandwiches
Savory Stone Fruit Hand Pies
Family Recipe Sweet and Salty Brittle
Cabernet Granita
Lemon Olive Oil Gelato

Estate Cabernet Sauvignon
Estate Red Wine
Fruit-Infused Water

Fashioning an Ice Bowl

Since serving gelato out of a gigantic block of ice isn't practical for most hostesses, Amy offers an equally fabulous alternative: creating individual serving bowls out of ice and flowers, fruit, or herbs.

1. Gather a pair of bowls, one that holds about 2 cups and the other about ½ cup. Flexible silicone and metal bowls work best.

2. Place ice chips in bottom of larger bowl equal to the desired thickness of the ice bowl. Place the small bowl on the ice chips and fill the gap with more ice, making sure inner bowl is level. Place decorative items such as flowers, herbs, or sliced citrus with the ice chips.

3. Weigh inner bowl down with rice, beans, or pie weights. Pour water in the gap between the bowls about a third full. Place the bowls on a flat surface in the freezer and freeze until solid. Repeat twice with layers of décor and water until the space between the bowls is frozen.

4. Loosen inner bowl by filling it with warm water and letting it stand about 1 minute. Remove outer bowl by dipping it in warm water. Wrap in plastic wrap and store in the freezer until ready to serve.

5. Repeat steps 1-4 to create more bowls.

6. Fill bowls with gelato and serve immediately. On warm days, place bowl on a small serving plate topped with flowers and herbs to keep ice bowl from sliding around.

Opposite, clockwise from top: Gelato service included Candied Lemon Slices, sea salt, and estate olive oil for garnish. Various pitchers of water infused with fruit, herbs, and nasturtium petals provided a refreshing and beautiful alternative to wine. A breathtaking ice block presentation of gelato and granita was the highlight of the party.

Lemon Olive Oil Gelato with Candied Lemon Slices

Makes 1 quart

1¾ cups whole milk
¾ cup heavy whipping cream
1 teaspoon lemon zest
6 large egg yolks
½ cup sugar

¾ cup good quality extra-virgin olive oil
Decorative ice bowls
Flaked sea salt
Chopped fresh rosemary
Candied Lemon Slices

Combine milk, cream, and lemon zest in a non-aluminum saucepan over medium-low heat. Simmer until mixture is heated through, stirring constantly. Remove from heat and set aside. Cool to room temperature.

Process egg yolks and sugar in a blender or food processor for 30 seconds or until well blended. Add milk mixture gradually to egg mixture, processing constantly. Add olive oil gradually, processing constantly.

Pour water to depth of 1½ inches in bottom of a double boiler over medium-high heat. Bring to a boil; reduce heat and simmer. Pour custard into top half of double boiler; set over simmering water. Cook for 5 minutes or until mixture reaches 160 degrees and coats back of a spoon, stirring constantly.

Pour custard mixture into a medium bowl. Let stand to cool, stirring occasionally. Refrigerate for several hours or until well chilled. Freeze custard in a gelato or ice cream maker with gelato attachment according to manufacturer's directions. Transfer to a metal loaf pan; cover with plastic wrap and freeze for 1 hour.

Scoop into decorative ice bowls, if desired, and garnish with sea salt, rosemary, and Candied Lemon Slices.

CANDIED LEMON SLICES

2 organic Meyer lemons, sliced ⅛ inch thick
2 cups sugar

2 cups water

Remove seeds from lemon slices. Cook lemons in boiling water to cover for 1 minute. Remove slices with a slotted spoon and drain on paper towels.

Cook sugar and water in a large skillet over medium heat until sugar dissolves, stirring constantly. Add lemon slices. Reduce heat to low; simmer for 30 minutes or until soft and translucent. Remove slices to a silicone baking mat or parchment paper and let stand until dry. Cover and store in an airtight container in the refrigerator until ready to serve. Reserve lemon syrup for other uses. Makes about 1½ cups.

Hiking and Foraging Among the Vines

A visit to Palmaz Vineyards is typically spent underground, learning about the winemaking process and marveling at the scale and scope of the facility. This state-of-the-art winery is housed in eighteen levels of caves that are carved into the hillside. More than a usual tasting, visitors here embark on an epicurean adventure of wine and food pairing, as well as an education in winemaking technology.

One summer morning, however, proprietor Florencia Palmaz invited a small group of visitors to join her outdoors, rather than underground, to take an experiential hike through the vineyard and forage for snacks along the way. "Being among the vines and picking fruit gives you a different perspective on the art of winemaking," says Florencia.

An abundant fig tree near the muscat vineyard was their first stop. Here, the group picked plump figs and harvested bunches of muscat grapes to create their own breakfast parfaits. Sipping chilled Florencia Muscat, they enjoyed the rare opportunity of tasting the finished wine and grapes together.

A brisk walk up a vineyard lane led the hikers to the vegetable garden, where they selected tomatoes, cucumbers, and fresh herbs to eat on bread slathered with sweet Easy Homemade Butter. Ice water infused with lemon and cucumber quenched their thirst.

From there, Florencia led them to her favorite spot at the crest of the hill, with its sweeping views of the vineyard and surrounding hills. Hiding among the vines was a tub filled with ice, jars of Cabernet Chicken Salad, and bottles of Lavender Lemonade. Guests picked cabernet berries to add some sweetness to their salads.

Hiking up to the winery caves, they were rewarded with a cool glass of chardonnay and Smoked Salmon Stars. Then, the group descended several levels into the cellars for a rare treat: tasting cabernet from the barrel. To help temper the tannin in the young robust cabernet, Palmaz served Piave Gougères with Prosciutto.

Touched by the unique experience, Florencia's guests left with rich memories and a deeper, more tangible understanding of the winemaking process. "As they say," Florencia explains, "it all begins in the vineyard."

Opposite: Guests hiked from station to station in the vineyard, foraging for snacks and taking in the exquisite property. Below: A striking yet deceiving structure serves as the façade to Palmaz's eighteen-story, 100,000-square-foot underground complex.

Left and below: Muscat wine was served with European-style yogurt. Fresh figs, hazelnuts, granola, honey, and muscat grapes were ingredients in creating parfaits for breakfast. Opposite: Hikers picked tomatoes and other vegetables to enjoy with Easy Homemade Butter on artisan bread.

Easy Homemade Butter

Makes 1 cup butter and 1 cup buttermilk

Enjoy this deceptively easy homemade butter with fresh rustic bread along with ripe tomatoes, cucumbers, and herbs picked fresh from the garden.

2 cups heavy whipping cream

½ teaspoon large flaked sea salt or kosher salt

Line a colander with 3 or 4 layers of cheesecloth; place over a bowl and set aside. Pour whipping cream into a large mixing bowl. Beat at medium-low speed with an electric mixer until slightly thickened. Increase speed and beat until stiff peaks form. Beat until mixture breaks up and butter and liquid separate.

Transfer mixture to colander, pressing butter against the cheesecloth to squeeze out all of the buttermilk. Pour buttermilk into an airtight container and refrigerate for up to 2 weeks.

Place butter on a flat surface and fold in sea salt until evenly mixed. Transfer to a shallow dish. Serve immediately or cover and refrigerate for up to 2 weeks.

Lavender Lemonade

Makes 8 (16-ounce) bottles

3 cups sugar
3 cups water
1 cup dried edible lavender flowers
 Peel from 5 Meyer lemons

1½ cups Meyer lemon juice
8 (16-ounce) glass bottles with swing-top caps
 Distilled water

Combine sugar and water in a saucepan over medium-high heat. Bring to a boil. Reduce heat and simmer for 5 minutes. Remove from heat and stir in lavender and lemon peel. Steep for 30 minutes; cool to room temperature. Strain through a fine mesh sieve into a bowl.

Add lemon juice to infused syrup mixture and stir to mix. Pour mixture evenly into bottles. Top off with distilled water. Seal and refrigerate until ready to serve or for up to 2 weeks.

Pictured on page 37.

"I cook to relax and love to gather people together. Delicious food and wine are what I use to lure them in. For me, so many of life's great moments happen around the table."

—FLORENCIA PALMAZ

Florencia Palmaz

Born in Argentina, Florencia's love of food and wine began as a college student in Texas. This passion led her to partner with her mother in establishing GoodHeart Brand Specialty Foods Co. This San Antonio–based company produces high-quality foods for professional chefs and home cooks. Florencia splits her time between Texas and her family-run winery in California, which she cofounded in 1997. A culinary force, Florencia recently authored the award-winning cookbook *At the Table and Around the Fire.*

Menu

Muscat and Fig Parfaits
Florencia Muscat

Garden Toast with Easy Homemade Butter
Cucumber Lemon Mint Water

Pick-Your-Own Cabernet Chicken Salad
Lavender Lemonade

Smoked Salmon Stars
Amalia Chardonnay

Piave Gougères with Prosciutto
Barrel Sample of Cabernet Sauvignon

Pick-Your-Own Cabernet Chicken Salad

Makes 4 lunch servings or 8 appetizer servings

- 2 cups shredded rotisserie chicken breast
- 1 cup finely chopped celery
- ½ large shallot, finely chopped
- 2 tablespoons chopped fresh chives
- 1 tablespoon chopped fresh tarragon

- Buttermilk Yogurt Dressing
- Freshly ground pepper to taste
- 1 cup cabernet berries (grapes) or fresh pomegranate arils

Combine chicken, celery, shallot, chives, and tarragon in a large bowl. Stir in Buttermilk Yogurt Dressing and sprinkle with pepper. Divide chicken salad among 1- or 2-cup hinged canning jars and garnish with cabernet berries. Seal and refrigerate until ready to serve.

BUTTERMILK YOGURT DRESSING

Makes 1 cup

- ½ cup buttermilk
- ½ cup plain Greek yogurt
- 1½ teaspoons olive oil

- 1 small garlic clove, lightly crushed
- Salt and freshly ground black pepper to taste

Whisk buttermilk, yogurt, olive oil, and garlic in a bowl. Whisk in salt and pepper. Cover and chill for 8 hours or overnight to allow flavors to blend. Remove garlic before serving.

Above: At the crest of the vineyard, hikers picked cabernet berries from the vine to add sweetness to their Cabernet Chicken Salad. Right: Refreshing Lavender Lemonade on ice.

Smoked Salmon Stars

Makes about 3 dozen

This is by far the most popular hors d'oeuvres at the winery. Nicolas, my 7-year-old, sneaks into the kitchen to steal them from the counter as they are being prepared. Wasabi caviar is a wonderful freezer staple; use it on canapés, deviled eggs, or tuna tartar.

10–12 slices sourdough bread
    6 ounces cream cheese, softened
    ½ small red onion, minced

1 pound cold smoked salmon, julienned
2 ounces wasabi caviar

Preheat oven to 375 degrees. Cut crusts from bread and cut each slice with a star-shaped cutter, or cut each slice into quarters to form triangles. Place on a rimmed baking sheet and bake for 15 minutes or until golden brown. Cool completely on a wire rack.

Spread about 1 teaspoon cream cheese on each star and sprinkle with a small amount of red onion. Top each with a portion of salmon and a small dollop of caviar.

Stealing Wine from the Barrel

If you spy a wine "thief" when visiting a winery, don't call the police—say, "Yes, please!" A wine thief is a long glass pipette that is used to "steal" wine from the barrel for testing at different stages of the aging process. Being offered a sample of wine from the barrel is a gift that few visitors to Napa Valley are able to experience. If you get this opportunity, accept it! For those who are unaccustomed to drinking young wine in an unfinished raw form, the wine may be less smooth or beguiling. The lesson is in learning to taste beneath the oak and identifying the flavors of fruit. Try tasting the stolen wine first. Then, follow it with the same bottled wine to discover how it evolves over time.

Opposite: Florencia greeted hikers at the winery with Smoked Salmon Stars and glasses of chilled chardonnay. Top: A wine thief is used to extract wine from the barrel. Left: Cabernet sauvignon was served with gougères and prosciutto.

Constant Culinary Delights

The town of St. Helena has protected its historic buildings, preserving the feel of a timeless small town. Back in the 1890s, the old stone Esmeralda Winery stood just outside of town. This former winery is now integrated into a residential neighborhood and is the "city" home of Mary Constant.

On a lovely fall evening, Mary, in her usual flair, invited guests to join her for a home-cooked al fresco supper in the olive grove. Cement tables were set in an understated and elegant way, with elements from the garden incorporated into the centerpieces. A ribbon of greenery accented with just-picked lemons and hydrangeas ran down the table. In lieu of a traditional tablecloth, Mary used a plain beige painter's drop cloth she picked up at the local paint store. "It's the perfect benign base," explains Mary. "I don't worry if someone spills red wine on it." Silver julep cups used as water glasses, a jumble of sterling flatware, and stunning Astier de Villatte plates added a touch of sophistication to each place setting.

For that evening's dinner, Mary cooked tender California Short Ribs and polenta to pair with CONSTANT Cabernet Sauvignon, Freddy's Cuvée. A largely self-taught chef, Mary says she started cooking out of necessity. "Actually," she says, "it was out of self-preservation. My mother was a terrible cook. I didn't know a good egg until I got to college." After discovering what great food was, she learned to create it. Her culinary pursuits escalated when she and her late husband, Freddy, founded CONSTANT Diamond Mountain Vineyard in 1993. While Freddy made wine, Mary found herself spending much of her time in the kitchen, preparing lunches and dinners and creating food pairings for wine tastings and events in their home.

Dinner with Mary that night was a culinary delight. Here, authentic food was made and served with love and laughter. It was also a lesson in understated elegance with a touch of whimsy—in every way, a perfect evening surrounded by the warmth of friendship.

Below: Built in the 1890s, the historic stone Esmeralda Winery made wines exclusively for the Palace Hotel in San Francisco. In the 1970s, the winery was converted to a residence that is now the home of Mary Constant. Opposite: Roses, jasmine, and bougainvillea cascade out of a wire basket in the garden.

Mary Constant

A fifth generation Californian, Mary's great-great-grandfather was a California 49er looking to strike gold. Mary came to Napa Valley in 1993, when she founded CONSTANT Diamond Mountain Vineyard with her late husband, Freddy. An avid cook and entertainer, Mary is an inductee into Les Dames d'Escoffier, a worldwide society of professional women of high achievement in the fields of food, fine beverage, and hospitality.

"Entertaining is sharing what I love to do: shop, cook, set a beautiful table, talk, and drink great wine. It's showing off my skills to people I love and friends I want to make."

—MARY CONSTANT

Left and top: Silver julep cups etched to commemorate different sailing adventures were used as water glasses. Above: A ribbon of white hydrangeas, limes, cabbage leaves, and winterberries ran down the center of the tables.

California Short Ribs

Makes 4 servings

I call this recipe California Short Ribs because of the addition of orange along with chocolate, reminiscent of Mexican mole. This combination of flavors creates a rich sauce that enhances the tender braised beef. It is a great recipe for large dinner parties because it can be made ahead.

3 tablespoons olive oil, divided
6 pounds beef short ribs, trimmed
    Salt and freshly ground pepper to taste
2 cups chopped sweet onions
1 cup chopped celery
1 cup chopped carrots
1 (750 ml) bottle dry red wine, such as
    Diamond Mountain Vineyard Cabernet
1 cup sweet vermouth

1 (14-ounce) can diced tomatoes
1 tablespoon tomato paste
1 tablespoon fresh thyme leaves
1 tablespoon finely chopped bittersweet
    chocolate
2 tablespoons orange zest plus more
    for garnish
⅓ cup orange juice
    Olive oil

Preheat oven to 275 degrees. Heat 2 tablespoons olive oil in a large Dutch oven over medium-high heat. Sprinkle ribs with salt and pepper and cook in batches for 10 minutes or until browned on all sides, turning occasionally. Transfer to a plate.

Drain drippings from pan and add remaining 1 tablespoon olive oil. Heat over medium-high heat. Add onions, celery, and carrots; cook for 4 to 5 minutes or until onions are translucent, stirring frequently. Transfer to a bowl.

Combine wine and vermouth in pan. Bring to a boil. Reduce heat and simmer for 10 minutes or until reduced by half. Stir in tomatoes, tomato paste, and thyme; bring to a boil.

Add reserved ribs and vegetables to pan. Add water, if necessary, just until the ribs are barely covered. Bake, covered, for 2½ hours or until meat and vegetables are tender. Transfer ribs to a bowl using a slotted spoon. Remove vegetables using a slotted spoon, discarding vegetables.

Skim fat from top of braising liquid. (You can refrigerate ribs and liquid separately overnight. Scrape away hardened fat from top of liquid. This reduces greasiness and improves flavor.) Bring liquid to a boil over medium heat. Reduce heat and simmer. Stir in chocolate, orange zest, and orange juice. Simmer for 5 to 7 minutes or until sauce is smooth and slightly thickened. Add ribs to sauce and cook until heated through. Garnish servings with orange zest, if desired.

Clockwise from top: Mary showed her sense of humor on her cocktail napkins. CONSTANT Cabernet Franc. The olive grove provided a natural shade canopy. Opposite: Fresh orange zest added color to Mary's short ribs.

Coffee Hazelnut Bread Pudding

Makes 8 servings

- 1 (12-ounce) loaf brioche or challah bread, or 5 brioche rolls
- ¾ cup Nutella®
- 3 cups heavy whipping cream, divided
- 1 cup sugar
- 3 teaspoons instant espresso or powdered instant coffee, divided
- 3 large eggs

Preheat oven to 350 degrees.

Slice bread thinly and spread half the slices evenly with Nutella®. Top with remaining bread slices and cut into 1-inch squares. Arrange tightly in a buttered 8x8-inch baking dish.

Combine 2 cups cream and sugar in a saucepan over medium heat. Cook for 2 to 3 minutes or until sugar dissolves, stirring constantly. Stir in 2 teaspoons espresso. Remove from heat.

Beat eggs in a medium bowl. Whisk in ½ cup warm cream mixture. Add remaining cream mixture gradually, whisking constantly. Pour custard over brioche squares, pressing to distribute liquid. Place baking dish in a deep roasting pan. Fill the roasting pan with hot water to a depth of 1 inch. Bake for 45 minutes.

To serve, beat the remaining 1 cup whipping cream until soft peaks form. Serve over each serving of bread pudding. Sprinkle lightly and evenly with the remaining espresso powder or with freshly grated chocolate.

Get Organized. Enjoy the Party.

Having thrown hundreds of dinner parties, Mary has learned a lesson: to really enjoy a party and spend time with guests, be organized. "Otherwise," says Mary, "you won't be at the table; you'll be in the kitchen."

Here are Mary's tips on how to be prepared.

- Make a list of everything you need to do a week in advance. Start by writing out the menu, including hors d'oeuvres, and then detail what each dish needs, from ingredients to plates.

- Do as much in advance as possible. If a soup or pasta or sorbet can be frozen, make it a week before.

- Lay out everything needed for service the night before. Decide what plates, flatware, and glasses will be used for each dish and put them out. Take a visual inventory. If you are dining indoors, set the table.

Opposite: The jumble of silver placed at each setting was like a game of pick-up sticks. Mary let her guests decide what knife or fork to use. "They don't care about using the right one anyway," she laughs. Above: Shaved dark Valrhona chocolate added decadence to the Chocolate Hazelnut Bread Pudding.

Chief of Crustaceans

During the summer months, many Napa Valley wineries host indulgent feasts, where dozens of guests don a bib and eat lobster, prawns, sausages, and vegetables with their hands. This seemingly uncouth dining experience is a trend that truly indoctrinates guests into the Napa Valley lifestyle.

The mastermind behind these ubiquitous lobster feeds is Chef John Sorensen, also St. Helena's fire chief. One August evening, John hosted an "intimate" feast (in his mind, fewer than twenty guests) at Stag's Leap Wine Cellars, alongside picturesque Fay Lake. The lakeside lawn and beach were an idyllic setting for a crustacean banquet—and Stag's Leap wines were the perfect accompaniment.

John's dinner was simple yet indulgent. Little effort was required to set the table. There were no knives, forks, or plates. Just bibs, cloth napkins, and sets of lobster crackers. All of the ingredients went into one pot. The key to cooking was precision timing. John was a clock-watcher, adding each element precisely at the right minute so that every item—from artichokes and onions to lobster and prawns—was cooked to perfection.

John poured the repast straight from the pot onto the middle of the table, making the meal the centerpiece. With bibs and tools in hand, guests delved into the bounty, dipping bites into drawn butter and adding spices like Slap Ya Mama Creole Seasoning. Once guests were satiated, they used warm, damp towels to freshen up and took a short stroll around the lake, under a sky dotted with cotton ball clouds.

The cleanup was as simple as the setup. "I laid waxed butcher paper on the table so I could roll up the detritus," says John. "The heavier waxed paper doesn't break down when it gets wet."

Guests returned to the table after their walk to enjoy a slice of tangy Lemon Cheesecake with fresh berries prepared by Mama Ines, John's number one baker. John added the lobsters he prepared that evening to his ongoing tally: in the summer of 2016, he cooked 15,685 lobsters.

Opposite: Whole Maine lobster was the centerpiece for this crustacean feast. Below: With striking views of the Palisades and the "Stag's Leap," Fay Lake at Stag's Leap Wine Cellars was a stunning setting for an al fresco summer meal.

John Sorensen

A chief, chef, and butcher, John Sorensen grew up in Napa Valley. He attended St. Helena High and worked at Keller's Meats, the local butcher shop. He eventually became the butcher of Keller's Meats before opening his own catering operation, specializing in lobster feeds, barbecue, and pizza. A true local hero, John has been a member of the fire brigade for twenty-seven years.

Above: John's chief's helmet weighs five pounds. Right: The supper made a colorful and impressive centerpiece. Opposite: Lobster crackers, a bib, and a good napkin were the only utensils needed for this hands-on feast. After dinner, however, guests used a fork to eat their Lemon Cheesecake.

Menu

Whole Maine Lobster

Louisiana Hot Links

Whole Prawns

Corn on the Cob

Castroville Artichokes

Roasted Garlic

Sweet Yellow Onions

New Potatoes

Sourdough Bread

Mama Ines's Lemon Cheesecake

Karia Chardonnay

Artemis Cabernet Sauvignon

Mama Ines's Lemon Cheesecake

Makes 8 servings

1 cup graham cracker crumbs

1¼ cups sugar, divided

3 tablespoons butter, melted

3 (8-ounce) packages cream cheese, softened

1 tablespoon vanilla extract

3 large eggs

½ cup heavy whipping cream

Meyer Lemon Curd

Fresh berries

Preheat oven to 350 degrees. Butter a 9-inch springform pan lightly; cut a circle from parchment paper and place on bottom of pan. Combine graham cracker crumbs, ¼ cup sugar, and butter in a medium bowl. Press onto bottom of prepared pan. Bake for 10 minutes. Cool on a wire rack.

Beat cream cheese until light and fluffy. Add remaining 1 cup sugar and vanilla; beat until blended. Add eggs, one at a time, beating well after each addition. Add the whipping cream, beating constantly. Pour over crust.

Bake for 15 minutes. Reduce oven temperature to 300 degrees and bake for 45 minutes or until center barely moves when pan is touched. Turn off the oven and remove cheesecake. Run a knife around outside edge of cheesecake. Return cheesecake to oven, and partially open oven door. Cool cheesecake for 1 hour in oven. Remove and cool completely on a wire rack. Cover and chill for 8 hours. Spread Meyer Lemon Curd on top and serve with fresh berries.

MEYER LEMON CURD

2 large eggs

½ cup sugar

1½ teaspoons Meyer lemon zest

½ cup Meyer lemon juice

4 tablespoons butter, cut into pieces

Combine eggs, sugar, and lemon zest in a medium non-aluminum saucepan; whisk until smooth. Add lemon juice and cook over medium-low heat for 5 minutes or until mixture thickens, whisking constantly. Add butter, stirring until melted and well blended. While hot, cover surface with plastic wrap, pressing directly onto surface. Refrigerate for 3 hours or until well chilled. Makes 1⅓ cups.

Farm to Truck to Table

Cyclists visiting Napa Valley always find their way to Velo Vino. A pre-ride espresso, gourmet snacks, cycling gear, and route maps from Velo Vino get them out on the road. Clif Family wines and farm-fresh cuisine from the Bruschetteria Food Truck bring them back.

One balmy July evening, friends were invited to a casual "cycle to feast" on the patio of Velo Vino. Hosted by Gary Erickson and Kit Crawford, owners of Clif Family Winery, the supper was created from the day's harvest from the Clif Family Farm and inspired by Italian roadside meals from Gary and Kit's travels. From the kitchen of his Kelly-green food truck, Chef John McConnell fashioned an exquisitely simple and delicious family-style meal. He passed trays of bruschetta, bowls of colorful salads, and platters of perfectly roasted organic chicken out the kitchen window to be placed on the table.

The tablescape mirrored the dinner's organic ingredients. Natural linen napkins, a flour sack table runner, and hand-thrown ceramics served as a neutral base. Whimsical, colorful, and edible arrangements were made from flowers, herbs, and vegetables picked on the farm. "I love pops of color," says Kit—a sentiment that was also evident in the placement of bright orange, yellow, and purple pillows on the patio benches.

At the dinner table, a lively discussion about social responsibility evolved. Like a growing number of residents of Napa Valley, Gary and Kit are focused on sustainability. When they established their farm in 2004, they made a commitment to creating biodiversity—raising chickens as well as growing organic wine grapes, olives, fruits, and vegetables. The abundant crop fuels the food truck. It is also turned into preserves, oils, spices, and healthy snacks.

After supper, guests lingered around the firepit to sip Cold Springs Cabernet and savor a Chocolate Budino before jumping on their bikes to ride home. Carrying jars of Pluot Lavender Preserves and Meyer Lemon Marmalade from the farm, they left with full bellies, motivated to lighten their footprint on this earth.

Below: Velo Vino, in the heart of St. Helena, offers tastings of Clif Family wines and features an espresso bar, organic nibbles, gift items, and cycling gear. Guests who time their visit perfectly can enjoy lunch from the Bruschetteria Food Truck. Opposite: A bountiful basket of produce from the Clif Family Farm.

Summer's Market Salad

Makes 4 to 6 servings

Mix and match your favorite seasonal vegetables, like carrots in summer or Brussels sprouts in winter. You don't have to roast tender vegetables like yellow squash—just thinly slice and stir in with the vinaigrette.

- 2 small shallots, thinly sliced
  Sea salt to taste
- 3 small sweet onions, cut into wedges
- 8 ounces fresh small new potatoes, cut into wedges
- 8 ounces baby carrots or Brussels sprouts, peeled and halved
- 1 cup olive oil, divided

  Freshly ground black pepper to taste
- ¼ cup champagne vinegar
- 2 tablespoons Dijon mustard
- 1½ teaspoons honey
- 1 cucumber, quartered, seeded, and sliced
  Baby arugula
  Yellow squash, sliced
  Slivered almonds, toasted and chopped

Place shallots in a small bowl; sprinkle lightly with salt; set aside.

Preheat oven to 425 degrees. Place onions, potatoes, and carrots on a parchment-lined baking sheet. Drizzle with ¼ cup olive oil, tossing to coat. Sprinkle with salt and pepper. Bake for 20 to 40 minutes or until vegetables are golden brown, stirring occasionally and removing individual vegetables when tender but still holding their shape. Set aside to cool to room temperature. Transfer to a large shallow bowl.

Combine shallots, vinegar, mustard, and honey in a blender. Add the remaining ¾ cup olive oil, processing constantly. Add salt, processing constantly.

Stir cucumber into vegetable mixture. Stir in just enough shallot vinaigrette to lightly coat vegetables. Cover and refrigerate remaining vinaigrette for up to 2 weeks. Garnish vegetables with arugula, squash, and almonds.

Above: A radish was tied to each napkin, serving as both décor and an amuse-bouche. Flowers, herbs, and vegetables from the garden made up a bright and edible tablescape. Right: Summer's Market Salad.

"To us, the ideal party is a leisurely evening of good wine, food, and thoughtful conversation. We want our guests to unplug, slow down, and take pleasure in the simple things found in everyday life." —KIT CRAWFORD

Gary Erickson and Kit Crawford

A husband and wife team, Gary and Kit are the owners and co-chief visionary officers of Clif Bar. Founded in 1992 and named after Gary's father, Clifford, Clif Bar is centered around the philosophy that sustaining one's employees, community, and the environment is good business. Gary and Kit's passion for wine, love of farming, and desire to get closer to the earth brought them to Napa Valley to create Clif Family Winery and Clif Family Farm. They have received national acclaim for their innovative business model, which integrates social and environmental responsibility into every area of their business.

Menu

Bruschette
Pomodoro
Cured Salmon

Insalate
Summer's Market Salad
Fagioli e Grano

Roticceria
Pollo Arrosto

Dolci
Chocolate Budino

Vino
Rte Blanc Sauvignon Blanc
Grenache
Kit's Killer Cab Cabernet Sauvignon
Cold Springs Estate Cabernet Sauvignon

Peak-of-Season Pomodoro Bruschetta

Makes 4 servings

1 (16-ounce) loaf sourdough or other rustic bread
½ cup pitted kalamata olives
½ cup fresh lemon juice
1 tablespoon dried oregano
1 tablespoon Dijon mustard
1½ teaspoons red wine vinegar
$\frac{1}{16}$ teaspoon crushed red pepper flakes

½ teaspoon sea salt plus more to taste
1 cup extra-virgin olive oil, divided
4 assorted heirloom tomatoes, cored
1 small cucumber
1 garlic clove, halved
4 ounces burrata cheese, cut into pieces, or crumbled feta
Torn fresh mint leaves

Remove rounded ends of loaf and cut 4 (½-inch-thick) lengthwise slices. Set aside for several hours or overnight to dry (slightly stale bread will maintain crunchy texture).

Combine olives, lemon juice, oregano, mustard, vinegar, red pepper flakes, and ½ teaspoon salt in a food processor. Process until finely chopped. Drizzle in ¾ cup olive oil, processing constantly until well blended.

Cut tomatoes into ½-inch slices; sprinkle with salt and set aside. Peel cucumber and cut into quarters. Remove seeds and slice. Toss cucumbers in ⅓ cup olive vinaigrette and set aside. Chill remaining vinaigrette in refrigerator for up to 2 weeks.

Toast bread slices until golden brown (center should remain soft). Rub one side with garlic and brush evenly with remaining ¼ cup olive oil. Transfer toast, garlic side up, to a serving plate. Top evenly with tomato slices, cucumber slices, and cheese. Garnish with fresh mint. Serve immediately.

Opposite: Pomodoro Bruschetta. Clockwise from top: Radishes and carrots inverted in glass vases and anchored by split peas made a unique and edible arrangement. Heirloom tomatoes were a key ingredient in the dinner, along with an abundance of vegetables, fruits, and herbs from the garden.

Fagioli e Grano

Makes 8 to 12 servings

1 cup uncooked farro	½–1 teaspoon crushed red pepper flakes
1 cup uncooked fregola sarda or Israeli couscous	¼ cup fresh lemon juice
	Sea salt to taste
16 ounces broccoli rabe, trimmed	1 cup (4 ounces) crumbled ricotta salata or Cotija cheese
1 (15-ounce) can garbanzo beans, rinsed and drained	1 pint yellow and red cherry tomatoes, halved
1 large carrot, peeled and grated	Extra-virgin olive oil
4 tablespoons olive oil, divided	Sprigs of fresh thyme
2 small garlic cloves, minced	

Cook farro and fregola sarda in separate pans according to package directions; cool completely.

Cook broccoli rabe in boiling water in a pot for 2 minutes. Remove with tongs and plunge in ice water to stopping cooking process. Drain well, squeezing out excess moisture. Chop coarsely.

Combine farro, fregola sarda, broccoli rabe, garbanzo beans, and carrot in a large bowl. Add 1 tablespoon olive oil, tossing to coat.

Combine the remaining 3 tablespoons olive oil, garlic, and red pepper flakes in a small saucepan. Cook over low heat for 2 to 3 minutes or until garlic is light golden brown. Remove from heat and stir immediately into salad mixture. Stir in lemon juice and salt. Sprinkle salad with ricotta salata, cherry tomatoes, and a drizzle of extra-virgin olive oil. Garnish with fresh thyme.

Opposite top: Fagioli e Grano. Opposite bottom: A letterpress menu was set at each place. Left: A veteran of Michelin-starred restaurants, Chef John McConnell loves being in the driver's seat of his organic restaurant on wheels. Below from left: Guests enjoy a supper from the Bruschetteria Food Truck, along with Clif Family wines. A wine caddy with flowers, herbs, and Kit's Killer Cab.

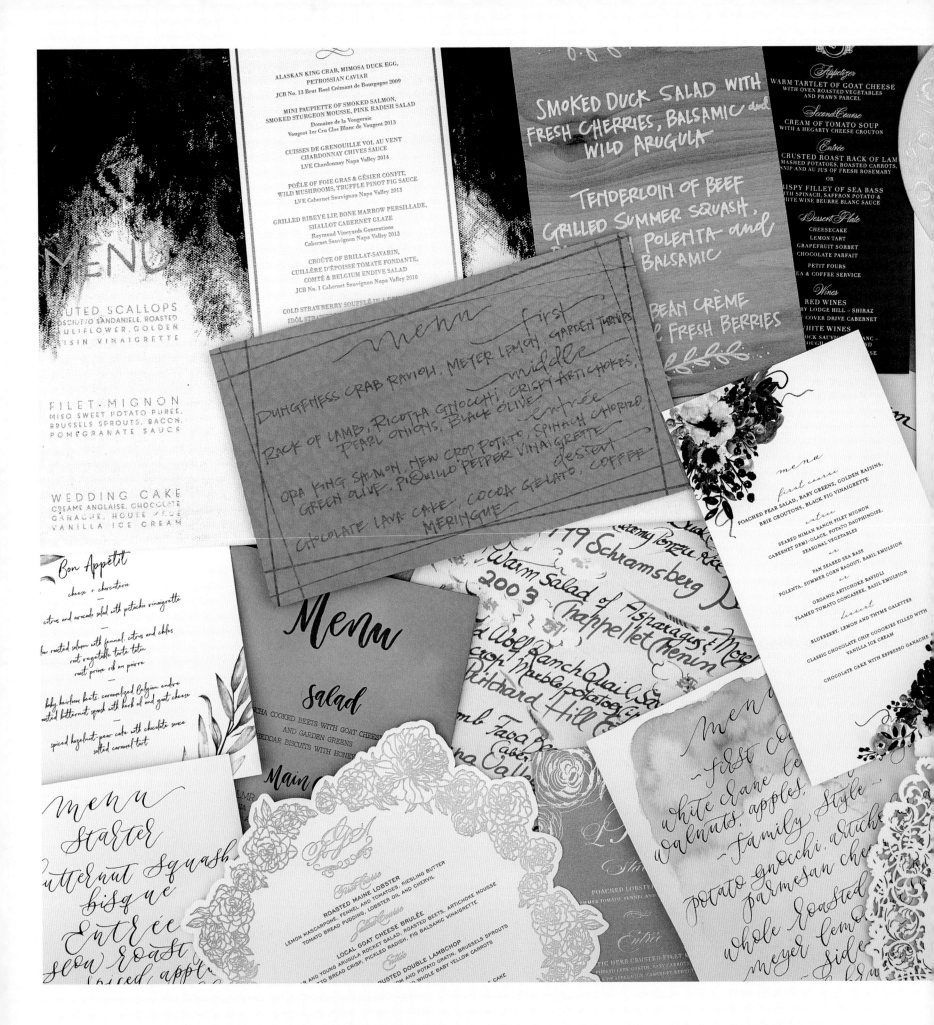

More than a Menu

When it comes to planning a party, most hosts think a great deal about the food they will cook and the wine they will serve. They focus, too, on what dishes, linens, candles, and centerpieces they'll use. What many hosts tend to overlook, however, is a printed menu—a guide to the meal—and how it can add to the guest experience.

A menu can enhance the festivities by setting a mood, supporting a theme, or creating a story. Consider how a unique presentation, creative wording, and interesting graphics could make a menu not only useful but memorable. Think beyond a flat rectangular page: a menu can be round, square, oversized, folded, or bound like a book. Don't be limited to paper: canvas, wood, leather, parchment, fabric, or a chalkboard can be fabulous. Graphics may be elaborate or simple, and words might be hand-painted, embossed, calligraphed, letter pressed, or printed. You might want to personalize a menu for each guest so it serves as both a place card and a menu. A unique menu can be a memento for guests to take home. No matter what form it takes, the menu is an important part of party décor.

It is hard to think about menus in the context of Napa Valley without remembering the late Margrit Mondavi. At Margrit's table, the menu was always a heartwarming and beautiful work of art. Inspired by the season and what was blooming and growing in her garden, she painted vegetables, flowers, and often a whimsical Bacchus on oversized pages, using her brush to scribe the various dishes and wines to be served. These menus, created with much love, were true treasures.

When hosting a party, think of Margrit and how she made each menu a gorgeous memento for her guests. Painting is not required, but creativity will certainly help make it more than just a list of food and wine.

A menu should be memorable and more than a guide to a meal. Make it part of the décor and a compelling piece that guests want to take home as a keepsake.

A Celebration of Summer

To enter the rustic yet elegant home of designer Barbara Colvin Hoopes is to be immersed in Napa Valley style. Featured in countless magazines and books, the home—comprised of four barnlike structures—was designed by notable architect Howard Backen and Barbara herself to capture the vistas of the valley and to pull the outdoors in.

On a July evening, Barbara invited an eclectic group of friends to join her for a unique Mediterranean-inspired dinner. After entering through the breezeway under tea lights hanging in glass globes, guests lingered in the entry courtyard to sip Hoopes wine and refreshing fruit drinks. They settled at a table clothed in white eyelet and participated in an informative cheese tasting with a prominent cheese writer.

Barbara likes to include an educational element for each party. "I want my guests to have an activity and to be inspired," she says. "It breaks the ice and provides a platform for conversation." She also loves to create a unique color palette for every event. After the cheese tasting, her guests moved to a fanciful, brightly hued dinner setting with tables clustered on a platform in the middle of the vineyard. Oranges and pinks decorated the tables, and sheer cream curtains blew dramatically in the breeze. The meal echoed the color scheme, starting with a vivid salad of yellow and orange nasturtium, hot pink watermelon radishes, and greens. The same brilliance was reflected in the yellow Lemon Triangles with Shortbread Crust and vibrant pink Fresh Fruit Sorbet for dessert.

Hand-embellished keepsakes were incorporated into the party—one of Barbara's signature touches. At the table, she included place cards stitched with each guest's name and menus with handmade tassels. Barbara, who hosts craft classes in her home, also made lifelike crepe paper lemons, radishes, and nasturtiums to rest on each napkin. These beautiful replicas represented important ingredients on the menu and were gifts for guests to take home.

The magic of this celebration of summer was more than ephemeral; Barbara's attention to detail and special touches left her guests with lasting memories and new friendships.

Below: Large pocket doors in Barbara's home open to create a seamless flow from the house into the vineyard. Opposite: Candles hanging on brightly colored ribbons and vintage benches with an eclectic array of decorative pillows greeted guests at Barbara's summer soirée.

Clockwise from above: A cleverly appointed back bar welcomed guests with Hoopes wine, refreshing beverages, potted herbs, and fruit. During a pre-dinner class, guests recorded their impressions about the cheeses they tasted. Garlic blossoms, nasturtium, and baby arugula added pops of color to each cheese plate. The evening's cheese tasting included Mediterranean white cheeses, such as Laychee and Labneh, from local producers.

Barbara Colvin Hoopes

A textile and women's fashion designer, Barbara moved to Napa Valley full time in 2003. After completing her own showplace home and receiving remarkable accolades, she launched her Napa design studio, Barbara Colvin & Co., to focus on all aspects of lifestyle design, from homes to headboards and carpets to clothes. Barbara fashions extraordinary homes across the country, using a comprehensive, expansive approach to creating beautiful environments. Her frequent travels inspire her passion for all crafts and creative pursuits and bring innovative ideas to her designs.

Menu

Meze
Beetroot Hummus, Tzatziki, Baba Ghanoush,
Olives, Pita
Watermelon and Lime Cooler

Horiatiki Salad

Mediterranean Sea Bass

Lemon Triangles with Shortbread Crust
Fresh Fruit Sorbet Flowers
Chocolate, Strawberries, Blackberries,
and Mango

Hoopes Family Wines

"Entertaining is one of my favorite forms of self-expression. It is a chance to experiment, to share current interests, and to create a memorable experience with people whose company I enjoy." —BARBARA COLVIN HOOPES

Horiatiki Salad

Makes 8 servings

Horiatiki is Greek for seasonal fresh vegetable salad. Our salad includes what we found in the garden in July, but you may use any combination of sliced fresh vegetables and edible flowers.

½ cup olive oil
¼ cup red wine vinegar
1½ teaspoons Dijon mustard
1 small garlic clove, minced
Salt and freshly ground pepper to taste
6 cups baby gem lettuce

Fresh vegetables and flowers, such as cherry tomatoes, radishes, cucumbers, Brussels sprouts leaves, nasturtium, oregano blossoms, and mustard blossoms
Feta cheese

Combine olive oil, vinegar, mustard, and garlic in a jar; cover and shake vigorously. Add salt and pepper. Cover and chill until ready to serve.

Shake the vinaigrette vigorously. Toss greens and vegetables with vinaigrette to taste. Arrange on individual plates or a serving platter. Top with flower blossoms and sprinkle with feta cheese.

Watermelon and Lime Cooler

Makes 8 cups

12 cups coarsely chopped seedless watermelon
½ cup fresh lime juice
Simple syrup or agave nectar, optional
Sprigs of fresh mint

Blend watermelon and lime juice in batches in a blender until smooth. Strain through a fine mesh strainer into a serving pitcher, discarding pulp.

Stir in simple syrup and chill until ready to serve. Serve over ice and garnish with mint.

Opposite: Sheer curtains, lanterns, and vibrant colors set the vineyard stage.

Left: A stunning salad of local produce, much of it from Barbara's garden, mirrored the table's color palette.

Lemon Triangles with Shortbread Crust

Makes 40 triangles

Shortbread Crust
1½ cups sugar
6 large eggs, at room temperature
1 tablespoon lemon zest

1 cup fresh lemon juice
½ cup unsalted butter, cut into pieces
¼ teaspoon kosher salt
Powdered sugar

Preheat oven to 350 degrees. Bake chilled Shortbread Crust for 15 to 20 minutes or until light golden brown. Cool on a wire rack.

Whisk sugar and eggs in a medium saucepan. Whisk in lemon zest and lemon juice. Cook over medium heat for 5 to 8 minutes or until mixture reaches 155 degrees and thickens slightly, stirring constantly. Add butter and salt and cook until butter is melted, stirring until mixture is smooth.

Pour lemon filling into baked Shortbread Crust. Bake for 10 to 15 minutes or until set but slightly soft in center. Cool completely on a wire rack. Cover and refrigerate for at least 4 hours.

Dust lightly with powdered sugar and cut into triangles. Transfer to a plate. May store in an airtight container in the refrigerator for up to 1 week.

SHORTBREAD CRUST

1 cup unsalted butter
½ cup sugar
2 teaspoons lemon zest

2 cups all-purpose flour
⅛ teaspoon kosher salt

Line a 9 x 13-inch baking pan with parchment paper; set aside.

Beat butter, sugar, and lemon zest at medium speed with an electric mixer until smooth. Beat in flour and salt. Press mixture over bottom of prepared pan. Cover and refrigerate for 30 minutes or until ready to bake.

Fresh Fruit Sorbet

Makes 8 servings

1½ cups water
1½ cups sugar
½ cup fresh orange juice
⅓ cup fresh lemon juice
1 quart strawberries, hulled

2 ripe mangos, peeled and chopped
1 tablespoon fresh lime juice
1 tablespoon superfine sugar
Fresh berries
Fresh mint

Combine water and sugar in a saucepan over medium heat; cook just until sugar dissolves. Cool completely and stir in orange juice and lemon juice. Purée strawberries in a food processor and stir into juice mixture.

Freeze sorbet in an ice cream maker according to manufacturer's directions. Transfer to a metal pan or spoon into sorbet molds and close tightly. Freeze until ready to serve.

Combine mangos, lime juice, and sugar in a food processor; process until smooth. Strain through a fine mesh strainer. Serve sorbet with mango sauce and garnish with berries and mint.

Left: A variety of handcrafted elements echoed the color scheme of the party—from the stitching on the place cards and the ribbons holding the tea lights to the lifelike crepe paper lemons and colorful tassels on the menus. Opposite: A Fresh Fruit Sorbet flower or fruit, made from Barbara's collection of antique molds, was the focal point of each dessert plate.

Charmingly Southern

What happens when a Southern boy falls in love with a Napa Valley native? Sometimes they aim to leave a legacy. Jamey and Michelle Whetstone spent the better part of five years meticulously restoring a nineteenth-century chateau and turning it into a full-time winery tasting salon that is a beacon for entertaining. During their visit to Whetstone, guests step back in time, where lively conversation, attention to detail, and a sense of understated hospitality rule the day.

Growing up, Jamey spent summers in the Lowcountry of South Carolina, where his grandparents had a small restaurant celebrating local seafood, vegetables, waterfowl, pork, and, of course, fried chicken. To honor that upbringing, the Whetstones invited friends over one warm August night for a fried chicken supper with all the trimmings. Guests were greeted with ice-cold mint juleps in the "lounge" set up on the chateau's front lawn—echoing the Southern tradition of welcoming folks with a refreshing beverage.

For dinner, Michelle styled a classic Charleston-inspired table, setting it with her grandmother's china, mismatched family silver, and vintage stemware. "I like to use our china rather than hide it in a cupboard, waiting for a special occasion," she says. "To me, every gathering is worthy of using 'the good stuff.' I want guests to feel part of something special." The floral arrangements were tall and airy, while artfully handwritten menus added a personal element to the table.

"My grandfather used to cook whole pigs, chickens, and a pot of sauce," recounts Jamey. He called upon his close friend, Chef Morgan Robinson of SMOKE Open Fire Catering, to create down-home comfort food with an upscale bent. "Morgan can cook just about anything," says Jamey, "so it was easy for him to recreate my childhood memories."

The energy behind Michelle's vision to get back to the basics also rang true, with thoughtful cocktails, great music, and delicious food and wine, sprinkled with sincere conversation in a gorgeous setting. Cheers to that!

Opposite: Southern-inspired flowers made a dramatic table for a family-style supper. Below: An 1885 stone chateau houses Whetstone's tasting salon. In the summer, visitors taste al fresco under majestic oak and cedar trees. In the winter, the cozy indoor lounge has a wood-burning fire. Visits are by appointment only.

Menu

Organic Buttermilk Fried Chicken
Shrimp and Anson Mills Grits
Napa Cabbage Slaw

Watermelon Salad

Silverado Trail Strawberry Shortcake

'Catie's Corner' Russian River Viognier
'Jon Boat' Carneros Chardonnay
'Walala' Sonoma Coast Pinot Noir

Organic Buttermilk Fried Chicken

Makes 4 to 6 servings

Fry chicken in batches to avoid overcrowding in the pan. Since dark meat takes a little longer to cook, fry those pieces first, then fry breasts and wings. If desired, coat lemon slices with flour mixture and fry until golden brown.

2 gallons water	1 quart buttermilk
2 cups plus 2 teaspoons kosher salt, divided	2 tablespoons fresh thyme leaves
6 garlic cloves, crushed	2 cups all-purpose flour
6 sprigs of fresh thyme	1 tablespoon garlic powder
1 organic lemon, sliced	1 teaspoon freshly ground black pepper
1 (4-pound) organic chicken, cut into 10 pieces	Rice bran oil or canola oil for frying

Combine water, 2 cups salt, garlic, thyme, and lemon slices in a large container, stirring until salt dissolves. Add chicken to brine; cover and refrigerate for 2 hours or overnight. Remove chicken from brine; pat dry with paper towels. Discard brine.

Combine buttermilk and thyme in a large nonmetal bowl; add chicken. Cover and chill for 2 hours or overnight. Drain chicken, discarding buttermilk mixture. Let stand for 30 minutes.

Combine flour, garlic powder, remaining 2 teaspoons salt, and black pepper in a large bowl. Fill a large deep cast-iron skillet or Dutch oven with rice bran oil to halfway up sides and heat to 350 degrees over medium-high heat. Coat chicken with flour mixture, shaking off excess. Arrange half the chicken pieces, skin side down, in skillet. Reduce heat to medium; cover and fry for 6 minutes. Remove lid and increase heat to high. Turn chicken, over and cook, uncovered, for 12 minutes.

Remove batches to a wire rack set over a baking sheet and place in a 200-degree oven to keep warm.

Jamey and Michelle Whetstone

In 2002, Jamey made the first vintage of wine under his own label while working at Turley Wine Cellars. Michelle was part of Chef Michael Chiarello's team, launching Bottega Ristorante and NapaStyle. The duo left their jobs in 2005 to build Whetstone. They have since cultivated a respected wine brand, renovated a historic winery, and are raising four children—all with grace and warmth.

Opposite, from top: Michelle greeted each guest with a mint julep and served crispy Fried Chicken. Below: The evening included Silverado Trail Strawberry Shortcake in a Mason jar, French-inspired florals, handwritten menus paired with an olive branch, and an outdoor lounge.

Swine
and Wine

Driving down Highway 29 in Rutherford, visitors often do a double take when they spot the five towering fountains in front of Alpha Omega winery. The water display draws guests in, and the exceptional single vineyard wines and hospitality make them lifelong devotees.

Every year, proprietors Robin and Michelle Baggett BBQ for hundreds of people at their winery and at charity events in Napa Valley, lending significant support to the arts, healthcare, and the community. Biblically, the words "Alpha Omega" mean the beginning and the end—but when it comes to parties with the Baggetts, Alpha Omega is famous for its swine and wine.

One September evening, Robin fired up his massive smokers and went hog wild. Robin—a lawyer by trade and certified BBQ judge and bona-fide cowboy on the weekends—takes his smoking and grilling seriously. Even with an intimate guest list of sixteen, he smoked an entire pig. There was method to his madness though: since grape harvest was in full swing, Robin wanted to treat the cellar crew to pulled pork sandwiches for lunch the next day.

Michelle loves gathering folks together to share in revelry. She always says a prayer and raises a glass in gratitude, and she often serenades guests with a sultry song or two. That evening, she created a stylish yet comfortable atmosphere, incorporating the rustic cowboy lifestyle by using wooden plates and mini cast-iron pots for beans on her tablescape. "I also paid homage to my Georgia roots by setting the table with large wooden bowls overflowing with fresh peaches—which added a pop of color," says Michelle. Aromatic bundles of sage, rosemary, and thyme on each napkin served both as décor and a gift for guests.

The evening was quintessential Alpha Omega: Robin in his element smoking meat, laughing, and telling stories, and Michelle ever grateful for friendship, the joy of living in Napa Valley, and all of life's blessings. It was relaxed, real, and full of fun, just like the Baggetts.

Below: During their tour and tasting experience at Alpha Omega, guests visit the tank room, barrel room, and vineyard terrace. Visitors usually find the fountains dancing in front of the farm-style winery to be as nearly as captivating as the wine! Opposite: For the Baggetts' party, the entire meal, from corn and beans to a whole hog and ribs, was cooked in a smoker.

Clockwise from right: Sunflowers and bowls of fresh peaches added color to the family-style dinner setting. A chalkboard dinner menu was set up near the Baggetts' ubiquitous "Smokin' Lounge" pig. Below: Bundles of garden herbs were a décor element and also a gift for guests.

Menu

St. Louis Spare Ribs

Foraged Hog

Lexington Red Slaw

Corn on the cob with Chili Butter

Smoked Peaches with Late Harvest

WINES

2013 Reserve Chardonnay
2012 Proprietary Red
2013 Cabernet Sauvignon
2006 ERA

SMOKIN LOUNGE

Robin and Michelle Baggett

An attorney and former general counsel for the NBA's Golden State Warriors, Robin has long been passionate about farming—and wine. He planted 800 acres in San Luis Obispo, founding Tolosa winery in 1998. His zeal for the wine business then brought him to Napa Valley, where he and his wife, Michelle, established Alpha Omega in 2006. A twenty-year marketing veteran working with luxury brands, Michelle uses her expertise to develop the couple's two wine brands.

"We favor refined casual dining because authenticity is important to us. Our family-style meals convey warmth and generosity and encourage conversation even among strangers. The menu, whether simple or posh, is always paired with a beautiful setting and, of course, wine."

—MICHELLE BAGGETT

Robin's Smoked Spareribs

Makes 10 to 12 servings

According to Robin, preparation and patience are the most important aspects of making great ribs. He is up at dawn and starts the smoker at least 5 hours before he wants to serve the ribs.

3 slabs trimmed St. Louis–style pork spareribs (8 to 9 pounds, or 36 ribs)
French's yellow mustard
Big Poppa's Money BBQ Rub
1½ cups apple juice
1½ cups water

Start smoker and establish temperature at 270 degrees.

Trim spareribs into an almost perfect rectangle, removing any excess fat and chine bones. Remove shiny membrane on the bony side of the ribs, using a paper towel to get a good grip.

With your hand, lightly coat one side of the ribs evenly with mustard to create a thin film of glue to hold the rub. Apply the rub, using the Money Rub shaker, lightly but completely covering one side of the ribs. Let sweat for 15 to 20 minutes and pat down rub. Turn ribs over and repeat the process.

Place the ribs vertically in a rib rack in the smoker with bigger bones down. Mix apple juice and water in a spray bottle. After 1 hour, spray the ribs every 30 minutes with the apple juice mixture to keep them moist. Using a ThermoWorks Thermapen, check the internal temperature, removing ribs when the temperature reaches no less than 190 degrees. Total cook time will be 3½ to 4 hours.

Remove from smoker, cover with aluminum foil, and let rest for 10 minutes before slicing. Rib meat should come clean off the bone with a slight tug of your teeth.

Serve with a variety of BBQ sauces, such as light and heavy tomato-base, vinegar-base, and mustard-base sauces, to let individuals select their preferences.

Note: Robin highly recommends Big Poppa Smokers for all of your smoking needs and only uses Big Poppa's Money BBQ Rub. The winner of major BBQ competitions across the United States, the rub is the perfect blend of spices with a slight hint of sweetness.

Robin's wood recommendations, in order of preference, are: pecan, apple, cherry, or hickory.

Lexington Red Coleslaw

Makes 10 to 12 servings

Because it pairs so well with BBQ and doesn't have any mayonnaise, Robin thinks this will be the best coleslaw you've ever tasted. The secret ingredient in this slaw is the celery seeds. Add a little cayenne pepper if you like some heat!

1 cup ketchup
½ cup apple cider vinegar
2 teaspoons celery seeds
1 teaspoon kosher salt
1 teaspoon coarsely ground black pepper
½ teaspoon cayenne pepper (optional)
2 (14-ounce) packages Fresh Express 3-Color Deli Cole Slaw

Whisk ketchup, vinegar, celery seeds, salt, pepper, and cayenne in a small bowl. Add cabbage to a large bowl. Add ⅓ of dressing gradually to cabbage, mixing thoroughly with hands. Taste and add additional dressing to taste. Let stand for 30 minutes, tossing occasionally. Cover and chill until ready to serve.

Left: The Baggetts graciously opened a library vintage of Alpha Omega's renowned Era Cabernet Sauvignon blend. Robin's Lexington Red Coleslaw paired perfectly with BBQ. Opposite: A good smoke ring is a sign of a perfectly smoked sparerib.

Menu

Robin's Smoked Spareribs
Foraged Hog
King City Pink BBQ Beans
Lexington Red Coleslaw

Smoked Corn with Chili Butter

Grilled Peaches with Late Harvest Reduction

Reserve Chardonnay
Proprietary Red
Cabernet Sauvingon
Era

King City Pink BBQ Beans

Makes 10 to 12 servings

When making his famous King City Pinks, Robin has two "musts": a heavy stockpot and true King City Pink beans. He special orders his beans from L.A. Hearne Company. This recipe is easily doubled for larger crowds.

1 pound dry King City Pink beans or Santa Maria Pinquito beans

3½ quarts water

½ pound sliced bacon, diced

3 ounces loose uncooked Mexican chorizo, Cacique brand preferred

2 teaspoons ground Hot New Mexico chile pepper, El Guapa brand preferred

1 teaspoon red pepper flakes

½–1 jalapeño pepper, diced (optional)

1 teaspoon salt

1 teaspoon freshly ground black pepper

1 (14-ounce) can petite diced tomatoes with green chilies, undrained

1 medium red onion, diced

1 medium yellow onion, diced

Place pink beans in a large pot and cover with water; bring to a low boil and cook for 1 hour.

Add bacon, chorizo, ground chile, red pepper flakes, jalapeño, salt, and pepper; continue to cook at a low boil for 1 hour, stirring occasionally. (Note: You will not drain beans. The soup is heartwarming.)

Stir in tomatoes, red onion, and yellow onion; return to a boil and keep at a low boil for 30 minutes, stirring occasionally. Reduce to a simmer and cook for 30 minutes or until beans are tender.

Below: Robin used bacon and a specific variety of beans to enhance the flavor of this classic BBQ accompaniment. Opposite: Corn on the cob got a kick from Michelle's spicy chili butter.

Don't Call It Grilling; It's Real Smoked BBQ

Robin Baggett takes his BBQ seriously and cooks only in the traditional way: low and slow over indirect heat. To him, grilling over coals is not true BBQ. He also follows strict rules about what cuts of pork and wood should be used.

Traditionalists like Robin prefer to BBQ spareribs. Since spareribs are more challenging to cook than baby back ribs, cooking them well is considered a true test of skill. "Anybody can cook baby back ribs and make them taste good," says Robin. And beef ribs are a no-no. The only acceptable cut of beef is brisket.

Just how these cuts of meat became sacred in the BBQ world is unknown. Robin believes it goes back to pre-Civil War days. The plantation masters got the best cuts of meats: the back loins and the hams. This is where the expression "high on the hog" came from. The plantation workers got the tougher cuts: shoulders or belly spareribs. They discovered, however, that hours of slow cooking with smoke turned these less desirable cuts into tender, juicy meats. They then added rubs and sauces to create even more flavor.

Smoked Corn with Chili Butter

Makes 6 servings

When Michelle makes her chili butter, she picks fresh peppers in her friend Piper's garden to dry and make chili powder. She highly recommends using fresh peppers. Since you can't pick a peck of peppers from Piper, pick them up at your local market or farmers' market, put them in a 200-degree oven for a couple of hours to dry them, and then chop in a grinder.

- 6 ears corn, unhusked
- ½ cup unsalted butter, softened
- 1–3 teaspoons freshly ground chili powder
- 1 teaspoon ground cumin
- ½ teaspoon dried oregano
- 2 tablespoons extra-virgin olive oil
- Coarse sea salt to taste

Soak corn in water to cover in a bowl for 2 hours; drain. Combine butter, chili powder, cumin, and oregano in a small bowl; set aside.

Peel husks away from corn, but do not remove. Brush away silks and discard. Brush corn with olive oil and sprinkle with salt. Arrange husks back over corn.

Prepare smoker according to manufacturer's directions. Smoke corn for 30 to 45 minutes or until tender. Peel back husks, leaving on to use as handles for eating. Tie husks in a knot, if desired. Spread butter mixture over hot corn.

Note: If desired, grill corn in husks over medium heat for 15 minutes, turning occasionally. Remove husks and brush with butter mixture.

Honoring
Your Guests

Oakville, California, is home to many venerable wineries. A relative newcomer to the area is B Cellars. The letter "b" along with the degree symbol "°" found in their logo refer to BRIX, a wine term that defines the optimal sugar/alcohol content in grape juice. Since its first harvest in 2003, B Cellars has received high praise for both its wines and its stunning estate. A visit to its caves, open-hearth kitchen, and culinary gardens goes beyond simple wine tasting; it is educational, satiating, and engaging.

Proprietor Duffy Keys, along with his business partner, Jim Borsack, invited a group of friends from his native San Diego to dinner at the winery one beautiful summer night. Greeting them with a refreshing glass of Juliana Vineyard Sauvignon Blanc, Duffy took them to the garden, where they helped Chef Derick Kuntz harvest blackberries and vegetables to be used in the meal. Then the guests toured the winery's 11,000-square-foot facility before sitting on the vineyard terrace for dinner.

Duffy spent most of his career in the luxury hotel business, where hospitality revolves around a guest's likes and needs. He says, "Entertaining is all about the individuals I'm hosting. I like to tailor a party to the guest of honor or group overall, preparing their favorite dishes, incorporating the colors they love, and, of course, pouring their favorite wine." Duffy does this in an organic way, making his guests feel at home and comfortable.

To personalize the evening, Duffy called upon a Pacific Ocean sunset for inspiration. The menu, florals, water goblets, candles, and pashminas draped on each chair all reflected the sky at day's end, and the blue-gray napkins captured a sense of the sea. These colors also carried through to the meal, with pops of yellow, orange, and red in the salad, pasta, and entrée.

Raising a glass to friendship and Duffy's new facility, the guests drank B Cellar's Heritage Cabernet as they watched the sun disappear over the Mayacamas. Feeling at home, they embraced the subtle details Keys had orchestrated to honor them.

Opposite: Florals, menus, and table accessories alluded to the colors of the sunset. Below: Visitors to the B Cellars Hospitality House—with its open kitchen, outdoor lounge, and croquet court—get a sense of being at someone's home.

"When entertaining, we think about the composition of the guest list, the reason everyone is gathering, and then create the atmosphere, menu, décor, and setting accordingly." —DUFFY KEYS

Duffy Keys

After two decades as a senior executive with Four Seasons Hotels and Resorts, Duffy joined business partner Jim Borsack in 2003 to co-found B Cellars. A decade later, they unveiled a remarkable winery, caves, and a hospitality house, which are testaments to the quality of their wines. With Keys's background in luxury lodging, guests immediately feel at home when visiting B Cellars.

Tomato and Watermelon Stacked Salad

Makes 6 servings

1 small seedless
watermelon

3 large yellow heirloom
tomatoes

1 large English
cucumber

¾ cup Tomato
Vinaigrette

8 ounces burrata
cheese, cut into
6 pieces

½ cup Pickled Red
Onion

½ cup Pine Nut
Crumble

18 small green and
purple basil leaves

Salt and freshly
ground pepper to
taste

Cut 4 (¼-inch-thick) slices from watermelon, reserving
remainder for other uses. Cut 3 circles from each slice,
using a 2-inch round biscuit cutter. Slice each tomato into
4 (¼-inch-thick) slices. Cut out centers, using same 2-inch
round biscuit cutter; discard peeling. Slice cucumber into
12 (¼-inch-thick) slices.

Spread 2 tablespoons Tomato Vinaigrette on each of
6 salad plates. Stack tomato, watermelon, and cucumber
on plates; repeat. Place 1 piece of burrata cheese on top
of each stack. Top each evenly with Pickled Red Onion.

Sprinkle each plate with Pine Nut Crumble and garnish
with basil leaves. Sprinkle with salt and pepper.

TOMATO VINAIGRETTE

1 cup yellow pear or cherry tomatoes

¼ cup sherry vinegar

1 teaspoon Dijon mustard

1 teaspoon honey

Salt to taste

½ cup extra-virgin olive oil

Combine tomatoes, vinegar, mustard, honey, and salt in a blender; blend until smooth.
Add the olive oil gradually, blending constantly until incorporated and thick. Makes
1⅓ cups.

PICKLED RED ONION

1 medium red onion, halved and sliced
into thin strips

⅓ cup sugar

⅓ cup water

⅓ cup white vinegar

⅛ teaspoon salt

Fill a large bowl with ice water. Place onion in the bowl and soak for 20 minutes. Drain
and pat dry; return onion to bowl.

Combine sugar, water, vinegar, and salt in a small saucepan over medium-high heat.
Bring to a boil, stirring until sugar dissolves. Remove from heat and pour over onions. Let
stand for at least 1 hour. Serve at room temperature or cover and refrigerate until ready
to serve or for up to 2 weeks. Makes 1 cup.

PINE NUT CRUMBLE

½ cup pine nuts

¼ cup panko breadcrumbs

¼ cup (1 ounce) freshly grated
Parmesan cheese

1 tablespoon chopped fresh tarragon

Preheat oven to 350 degrees. Place pine nuts on a baking sheet and bake for 8 minutes
or until golden brown. Transfer to a shallow bowl; cool. Combine panko and Parmesan
in a small bowl and spread mixture evenly on a parchment- or nonstick foil-lined baking
sheet. Bake for 8 to 9 minutes or until golden brown; cool.

Combine pine nuts, panko mixture, and tarragon in a food processor, pulsing until
coarsely chopped. Makes 1¼ cups.

Clams and Linguini

Makes 8 servings

1–1½ pounds fresh linguini, or 1 pound dried
    linguini
1 tablespoon olive oil
½ pound smoked pork belly or bacon, diced
1 white onion, cut into strips
3 garlic cloves, thinly sliced

4 cups Tomato Broth
¼ cup chopped mixed fresh herbs (parsley,
    tarragon, chives, and chervil)
    Salt to taste
3 pounds Manila clams, scrubbed
    Sprigs of fresh herbs

Bring a large pot of salted water to a boil over medium-high heat. Add pasta and cook for 1 to 3 minutes (fresh) or 9 minutes (dried) or until tender. Drain and keep warm.

Meanwhile, combine olive oil and pork belly in a large heavy-bottomed pot over medium-high heat. Cook for 8 minutes or until pork belly is crisp, stirring occasionally. Remove with a slotted spoon; set aside. Drain all but 2 tablespoons drippings. Cook onion in drippings over medium-high heat for 5 minutes, stirring occasionally. Add garlic; cook for 1 minute, stirring frequently.

Stir in Tomato Broth, pork belly, mixed herbs, and salt. Bring mixture to a boil; reduce heat. Add clams to the pot and simmer for 4 to 6 minutes or until clams open, shaking pot occasionally. Discard any clams that do not open. Divide linguini among 8 shallow pasta bowls. Top evenly with clams and liquid. Garnish with sprigs of fresh herbs.

TOMATO BROTH

2 tablespoons olive oil
1 white onion, diced
6 garlic cloves, crushed
4 cups coarsely chopped Roma tomatoes
    (1¾ pounds)

4 cups water
1 bay leaf
2 teaspoons kosher salt
½ teaspoon red pepper flakes

Heat olive oil in a large heavy-bottomed pot over medium heat. Add onion and garlic; cook for 5 minutes or until onion is translucent, stirring occasionally. Add tomatoes and cook for 5 minutes, stirring occasionally.

Stir in water, bay leaf, salt, and red pepper flakes. Bring to a boil; reduce heat and simmer for 30 minutes. Remove from heat, allowing mixture to cool slightly. Transfer to a blender in batches and purée until smooth. Strain through a cheesecloth-lined colander, pressing with the back of a large spoon; discard solids. Makes 4 cups.

Top: Chef Derick Kuntz joined guests in harvesting blackberries and vegetables. Left: The Heritage Selection Cabernet Sauvignon is a remarkable blend of fruit from Beckstoffer's Heritage Vineyards. Opposite: Fresh parsley, tarragon, and chives add color to Clams and Linguini.

Menu

Tomato and Watermelon Stacked Salad
Yellow Heirloom Tomatoes, Watermelon,
Burrata Cheese, Pine Nut Crumble
Dutton Ranch Chardonnay

Clams and Linguini
Smoked Pork Belly, Tomato Broth
Blend 24

Grilled New York Strip Loin Steak
Fingerling Potatoes,
Garden Vegetables, Blackberry Bordelaise
Star Cabernet Sauvignon

Dessert Cheese Plate
Smoked Goat Cheese, Barely Buzzed,
Seasonal Jam, Annette's Chocolates
Blend 25

Grilled New York Strip Loin Steak

Makes 6 servings

6 (8-ounce) New York strip steaks
Chocolate Espresso Steak Rub

Blackberry Bordelaise Sauce
Fresh blackberries

Rub steaks evenly on all sides with the Chocolate Espresso Steak Rub. Let stand at room temperature for 30 minutes.

Preheat the grill to high. Wipe the grill grate with an oiled cloth. Grill steaks for 4 to 5 minutes. Turn steaks over and grill for 3 to 5 minutes for medium-rare (135 degrees), 5 to 7 minutes for medium (140 degrees), or 8 to 10 minutes for medium-well (150 degrees). Transfer the steaks to a cutting board; cover with foil and let rest for 5 minutes. Slice the steak thinly. Serve with Blackberry Bordelaise Sauce and garnish with blackberries.

CHOCOLATE ESPRESSO STEAK RUB

1 tablespoon ground espresso powder
1 teaspoon unsweetened cocoa powder
1 teaspoon garlic powder
½ teaspoon light or dark brown sugar
½ teaspoon chopped fresh tarragon

½ teaspoon ground Espelette pepper or hot paprika
½ teaspoon kosher salt
½ teaspoon black pepper

Combine espresso, cocoa powder, garlic powder, brown sugar, tarragon, Espelette pepper, salt, and black pepper in a small bowl.

BLACKBERRY BORDELAISE SAUCE

1 tablespoon olive oil
1 large shallot, chopped
½ cup beef demi-glace*

¼ cup red wine
10 fresh blackberries

Heat olive oil in a small saucepan over medium heat. Add the shallot and cook for 3 minutes or until tender, stirring constantly. Stir in demi-glace and red wine. Simmer for 5 minutes or until the mixture is reduced by a third. Stir in blackberries and cook for 5 minutes or until berries are tender. Pureé with an immersion blender until smooth. Strain through a fine mesh strainer. Makes ½ cup.

*Demi-glace, also known as demi-glaze, is a rich beef stock–based sauce often used as a base for other sauces. Ask your local butcher or look for it in specialty gourmet shops.

Opposite: Roasted fingerling potatoes accompanied the New York Strip. Top: A mix of candles and candleholders added whimsy to the table. Above: Sunset orange menus were personalized with each guest's name. Left: Roses and ranunculus with toyon berries and olive branches spilled onto the table and conjured up the colors of sunset.

A Patient Artistic Endeavor

Climbing the mountains in Napa Valley gives visitors a bird's-eye view of the Valley and access to some of Napa's hidden-gem wine producers. At 1,200 feet above the Valley floor on Howell Mountain is Clark-Claudon, a small-production, family-owned boutique winery. Visitors to Clark-Claudon hike in the vineyard, enjoy the views, and sip exceptional cabernet sauvignon.

One fall evening, Laurie Claudon and her husband, Tom Clark, planned an al fresco vegetarian dinner atop the vineyard. It was a time of gratitude and celebration, as the grapes were picked and the baby wines were barreled down. For Laurie and Tom, making wine is an artistic endeavor that requires patience. They quietly watch the seasons unfold in the vineyard, evaluate the wines as they evolve in the barrel, and allow them to just rest in the bottle. "Winemaking is not recommended for anyone seeking instant gratification," says Laurie. "But when the time comes for us to share a finished product—our own work of art—the patience and anticipation are worth it!"

The background canvas for dinner featured 365-degree views and a fall vineyard. Laurie kept the tablescape subtle and relaxed yet sophisticated so nothing would obstruct the views or the lively conversation. Wanting to stay local and sustainable, she set a plank table decorated with ferns and pomegranates harvested on the property. Her menu was heavily focused on homegrown produce, from figs, apples, and salad greens to walnuts and honey. Tom and Laurie also honored their relationships with Napa purveyors and artisans, serving cheese and mushrooms from local producers and using plates and bowls hand thrown by local potters. Each guest went home with a jar of Laurie's homemade fig jam with rosemary.

That evening, everyone weighed in on what matters most to them in winemaking. Is it nature, art, science, or passion? The conclusion: it is the dance among them all that keeps winemakers going from season to season while also giving reason for gratitude and celebration!

Below: Visitors are invited to taste wine and hike in Clark-Claudon's certified sustainable vineyard and the surrounding estate, a wildlife preserve. Appointments are required. Opposite: Expansive views and stunning fall colors were the backdrop for an al fresco dinner.

Tom Clark and Laurie Claudon

Following their Peace Corps assignment, Tom Clark and Laurie Claudon came to Napa Valley in 1974 to raise a family, grow grapes, and make wine. They founded Clark–Claudon Vineyards in 1989, releasing their first vintage of cabernet in 1993. Since its inception, the winery has been a family affair and now includes three generations. Besides family and wine, Tom and Laurie's passions include hands-on philanthropy, nature, and sustainability.

"The perfect party is one where the host and the guests feel relaxed, comfortable, and free to be themselves as the conversation expands with humor, thoughtfulness, and expression."

—LAURIE CLAUDON

Crab Parcels

Makes 32 appetizer servings

8 ounces cream cheese, softened
½ cup sour cream
4 green onions, minced
¼ cup finely chopped yellow or red bell pepper
1 tablespoon seafood seasoning or to taste
1 teaspoon minced celery

1 teaspoon celery seeds
1 pound crab meat, drained and shells removed
1 (16-ounce) package frozen phyllo dough, thawed
½ cup butter, melted

Combine cream cheese, sour cream, green onions, bell pepper, seafood seasoning, celery, and celery seeds in a large bowl and mix well. Fold crab meat gently into cream cheese mixture with a spatula or your hands. Set aside.

Preheat oven to 350 degrees. Cut parchment paper into 32 (12x12-inch) squares.

Place 1 sheet of phyllo on a work surface. Brush lightly with butter and place another sheet on top. Repeat 2 more times to create 4 layers. Cut phyllo in half lengthwise and crosswise to form 4 rectangles, about 6x8-inch each. Place stacked phyllo in center of 1 parchment square. Insert into ramekins or muffin cups. Repeat with the remaining parchment paper and phyllo dough. Bake, in batches, for 5 minutes or until almost done but not browned.

Scoop 2 tablespoons crab mixture evenly into each cup. Lift parchment paper from each cup and bring edges together to form a bundle. Secure each with kitchen string.

Place bundles on a large baking sheet. Bake for 20 minutes or until heated through.

Above: Tom places birdhouses in the vineyard to entice pest-loving birds to nest. Guests enjoyed the Twenty Year Anniversary Estate Cabernet Sauvignon with dinner. Left: A hand-thrown plate holds a delicate Crab Parcel.

Fresh Greens Salad with Walnuts

Makes 4 servings

This easy but delicious recipe is adapted from one featured in *The Forest Feast* by Erin Gleeson.

8 cups baby salad greens
2 pears, cored and thinly sliced
1 cup walnuts, toasted and chopped
¼ cup pomegranate arils (seeds)
¾ cup extra-virgin olive oil

¼ cup fig-flavored balsamic vinegar
2 tablespoons soy sauce
2 tablespoons toasted sesame oil
½ cup (2 ounces) shaved pecorino
  Romano cheese

Arrange salad greens and pears on a platter or individual salad plates. Sprinkle evenly with walnuts and pomegranate arils.

Whisk olive oil, vinegar, soy sauce, and sesame oil in a small bowl. Drizzle over salad and top evenly with cheese. Store remaining vinaigrette in the refrigerator for up to 1 week.

Taking Honey from the Bees

There are many parallels between wine and honey. Making wine and harvesting honey are both ancient arts that date back to 5,000 BC. Like wine, honey is impacted by terroir, and flavor will vary based on the surroundings of the hive.

The number of "hobby" beekeepers in the US is growing with the slow food movement. The Clark-Claudon family keeps a strong colony of honeybees to pollinate their orchard and gardens. They understand that these miraculous little insects also produce the only food that contains all the substances necessary to sustain human life.

Conscientious consumers are now seeking locally produced honey as a natural substitute for sugar and for its medicinal benefits. The bee pollen found in raw honey can ward off infections, provide natural allergy relief, and boost overall immunity. Local honey producers can be found at farmers' markets and some grocery stores. Read the label and look for organic, raw, unfiltered, and 100 percent pure honey.

Opposite, from top: Wild Mushroom Ragout over Polenta was served on plates handcrafted by Will and Nikki Callnan of NBC Pottery in Napa Valley. Baby greens, pears, and walnuts in the salad were all grown on the property. Above: Tom Clark and his eldest grandson, Brandon Forgie, maintain the family's beehives.

Menu

Summit Lake Goat Cheese Crostini
Homegrown Figs, Honey

Crab Parcels

Fresh Greens Salad
Walnuts, Pears
Wild Iris Sauvignon Blanc

Wild Mushroom Ragout
Cabernet Sauce, Polenta
Twenty Year Anniversary Estate
Cabernet Sauvignon
Eternity Reserve Cabernet Sauvignon

Brownies with Mint

Wild Mushroom Ragout over Polenta

Makes 4 to 6 servings

4 tablespoons butter, divided
2 tablespoons extra-virgin olive oil, divided
1 large onion, diced, divided
2 celery stalks, chopped, divided
2 pounds mixed fresh wild or brown
    mushrooms (such as porcini, chanterelles,
    matsutake, or shiitake), sliced ¼ inch
    thick, divided
½ teaspoon salt, divided
4 garlic cloves, minced, divided
2 tablespoons all-purpose flour

1 cup cabernet sauvignon
    Mushrooms reserved from Mushroom
    Stock
    Chopped fresh parsley
    Freshly ground black pepper to taste
3 cups Mushroom Stock
1 cup polenta
½ cup (2 ounces) Taleggio, Brie or other
    semi-soft cheese, grated or cut into pieces
½ cup (2 ounces) shaved Parmesan cheese,
    divided

Combine 2 tablespoons butter and 1 tablespoon olive oil in a large saucepan over medium-high heat. Cook until butter melts, stirring constantly. Add half the onion and half the celery. Cook for 3 to 5 minutes or until tender, stirring frequently. Add half the fresh mushrooms. Cook for 2 minutes or until mushrooms soften, stirring frequently. Stir in half the salt and half the garlic. Cook for 2 minutes. Transfer to a bowl. Repeat with remaining halves of the butter, olive oil, onion, celery, fresh mushrooms, salt, and garlic. Return first half of mushroom mixture to pan.

Add flour to mushroom mixture. Cook for 2 minutes or until flour is incorporated into mixture, stirring constantly. Stir in cabernet sauvignon. Cook for 5 minutes or until liquid is reduced, stirring constantly. Stir in reserved mushrooms from Mushroom Stock and parsley. Season with pepper.

Bring Mushroom Stock to a boil in a large saucepan over medium-high heat. Add polenta gradually, whisking constantly. Reduce heat and cook until polenta is thickened, whisking constantly. (Polenta is ready when it leaves the sides of the pan while stirring and will thicken as it cools). Remove from heat and let stand until thickened but not cold.

Preheat broiler. Spread polenta in an ovenproof platter. Top with Taleggio and half the Parmesan. Broil for 3 minutes or until cheese is bubbly. Spoon mushroom ragout evenly over polenta using a slotted spoon. Sprinkle with remaining Parmesan. Transfer liquid from mushroom ragout to a bowl and drizzle over individual servings.

MUSHROOM STOCK

2 tablespoons extra-virgin olive oil
1 large yellow onion
6 cups cold water
2 garlic cloves, coarsely chopped
½ ounce (about 1/3 cup) dried mushrooms
½ (8-ounce) container fresh wild or brown
    mushrooms
2 bay leaves

1/16 teaspoon dried sage
1/16 teaspoon dried thyme
1 carrot, coarsely chopped
1 celery stalk, chopped
4 sprigs of fresh parsley
6 borage leaves
½ teaspoon salt

Heat olive oil in a large pot over medium-high heat. Add onion and cook until golden brown, stirring frequently. Add water and remaining ingredients. Bring to a boil. Reduce heat and simmer for 30 minutes.

Remove mushrooms; chop and reserve for ragout. Strain remaining stock through a cheesecloth-lined colander into a bowl. Return to large pot. Simmer until reduced to 3 cups. Makes 3 cups.

Opposite: Wild Mushroom Ragout in a cabernet sauce was served on a bed of polenta. Right from top: As part of the third generation, Paxton, Josephine, Trevor, Finley, and Brandon are fortunate to learn from their grandparents. Tiny stumps held each place card. Exotic mushrooms from the farmers' market were used in the ragout.

"The proper glass perfects the overall enjoyment of wine by bringing out the very best the wine has to offer. A glass helps balance the flavors with perception of fruit, minerality, and tannins."

—GEORG RIEDEL

Georg Riedel is the tenth-generation owner of Riedel Crystal, headquartered in Kufstein, Austria. He has spent a lifetime studying and educating others on how to entertain with glassware and how the size and shape of a glass impact the smell and taste of wine.

Selecting and Setting Stemware

There are thousands of different shapes, sizes, and levels of wine glasses, which can make it confusing to purchase—and use—stemware. There's also etiquette about where to set wine glasses on the table and what glasses to use for particular wines. To guide people through the maze of stemware, Georg Riedel, owner of Riedel Crystal and the world's foremost expert on the subject, provides some insight.

Purchasing Stemware

When purchasing glasses, Riedel says, "Buy what you drink. Purchase a set of stemmed glasses to match the wine you enjoy the most. That's the only glass you need!" If you enjoy cabernet sauvignon, purchase a set of bordeaux glasses. "You can always expand your collection as your interest in and appreciation for wine styles broaden," says Georg. For informal entertaining, consider glasses without stems.

Setting Stems on the Table

The photo below illustrates what shape of glass is most appropriate for popular Napa Valley wines and the order in which stems should be placed on the table. The rule of thumb is to work from right to left, setting the water glass above the knife and then placing the wine glasses to the left. Begin with the wine that will be served with the first course—in this case, sparkling wine—and then set the stem for the second course wine to its left.

Neighbors Helping Neighbors

Below: Visitors from around the world come to Napa on the first weekend in June to experience the magic of Auction Napa Valley. Opposite: At the show-stopping live auction, attendees celebrate a winning bid on a one-of-a-kind experience paired with a curated collection of wine.

Every year on the first weekend in June, Napa Valley rolls out the red carpet to welcome visitors to the ultimate party in wine country: Auction Napa Valley. Hosted by the entire community, this must-attend event offers wine, food, and exceptional hospitality. "Our vintners are known for welcoming visitors throughout the year—but auction weekend is the best of the best," says former chair K. R. Rombauer.

The auction began in 1981, the dream of visionaries like Robert and Margrit Mondavi. Nearly four decades later, Auction Napa Valley has eclipsed their expectations, investing more than $170 million in Napa County community health and children's education non-profit organizations from American Canyon to Calistoga.

The weekend festivities start on Thursday evening with intimate dinners in the homes or wineries of select vintners. Notable chefs—many Michelin Star rated—prepare meals paired with each winery's finest vintages. Attendees spend one-on-one time with the host vintner over supper and, on the following night, experience another exclusive dinner at a new winery.

A wine and culinary extravaganza takes place on Friday. The Valley's finest restaurants prepare dishes for sampling. Here, attendees may find The French Laundry chef

Thomas Keller passing Salmon Cornets, Cindy Pawlcyn of Mustard's Grill serving churros, or Masaharu Morimoto offering tuna tartar tacos. Dozens of wineries pour their current wines, and more than 100 vintners share unique blends of yet-to-be-released wine from the barrel. These "futures" are sold in case lots in a tote board–driven auction. The showstopper for the weekend happens on Saturday under the big tent, where celebrities from Oprah to Joe Montana are often spotted. In the tent, jaw-dropping bids—often topping a quarter of a million dollars—are placed on unique experiences and one-of-a-kind wine collections curated by elite Napa vintners. Stellar chefs, including Emeril, Pierre Gagnaire, and Francis Mallmann, have prepared the post-auction dinner. These three remarkable days capture a magic that can't be replicated—until the following year at Auction Napa Valley.

Churros with Mexican Dark Chocolate Sauce

Makes about 2 dozen

¼ cup sugar
¼ teaspoon ground cinnamon
1 cup water
½ cup unsalted butter
¼ teaspoon salt

1 cup all-purpose flour
3 large eggs
Vegetable oil for frying
Mexican Dark Chocolate Sauce

Combine sugar and cinnamon in a shallow bowl and mix well; set aside.

Combine water, butter, and salt in a small saucepan over medium-high heat. Bring to a boil and cook until butter melts, stirring constantly. Reduce heat to medium. Add flour all at once and stir vigorously until mixture forms a ball that pulls away from sides of saucepan. Remove from heat and cool slightly. Add eggs, one at a time, stirring vigorously until smooth. Spoon mixture into a pastry bag fitted with a star tip.

Heat 1 to 2 inches of vegetable oil to 350 degrees in a Dutch oven or large saucepan. Working carefully and quickly, pipe 6-inch lengths of batter into the hot oil, using a knife or kitchen shears to cut into pieces. Fry for 3 minutes or until golden brown and cooked through, turning once. Transfer to paper towels using a slotted spoon and drain for about 10 to 15 seconds. Roll in cinnamon-sugar mixture. Transfer to a platter and keep warm. Repeat with remaining batter. Serve with Mexican Dark Chocolate Sauce.

MEXICAN DARK CHOCOLATE SAUCE

1 (3.2-ounce) disk Mexican chocolate, or
   3 ounces semisweet chocolate, chopped
2 tablespoons cocoa powder

⅓ cup evaporated milk or half-and-half
2 tablespoons light corn syrup

Pour water to depth of 1½ inches in bottom of a double boiler over medium-high heat. Bring to a boil. Reduce heat and simmer. Combine chocolate, cocoa powder, evaporated milk, and corn syrup in top of double boiler; set over simmering water. Cook and stir until smooth and well blended.

Opposite: Hog Island Oysters is one of the many restaurants that prepare special dishes.
Beloved Chef Cindy Pawlcyn has been a part of Auction Napa Valley for over twenty years.
Pawlcyn's Churros with Mexican Dark Chocolate Sauce are a fan favorite. Clockwise from top:
Harlan Estate wine, in three-liter bottles, was up for auction on Saturday. Dozens of vintners
pour their wine for guests. Tote boards were used to record bids for unique lots of wine
"futures." More than 100 vintners sample their barrel lots up for sale.

Clockwise from above: Known for his rustic open-fire cooking technique, Argentine chef Francis Mallmann's "kitchen" was a theater for auction guests. Paper lanterns decorated the ceiling of the reception tent. *Sports Illustrated* swimsuit model Kate Upton places a bid. Opposite: Attendees experience the frenzy of bidding and the elation of winning a coveted auction lot.

Napa Valley Vintners

Over 500 winery members host Auction Napa Valley annually. They join together to throw private parties and offer exclusive lots of wine and experiences for sale in the live, barrel, and "e" auctions. Each year, the event is led by one winery. Past chairs include the Opus One Team, Jeff and Valerie Gargiulo, David and Kary Duncan of Silver Oak Cellars, Agustin and Valeria Huneeus of Quintessa, and the Staglin, Chappellet, and Rombauer families.

"Guests marvel at the amazing one-of-a-kind auction lots and over-the-top hospitality they experience. Funds raised at the Auction create miracles for those in our community who need our help." —2013 AUCTION CHAIR GAREN STAGLIN, STAGLIN FAMILY VINEYARDS

Above: An elegant table was set for dinner with proprietors Agustin and Valeria Huneeus at Quintessa. Opposite, clockwise from top: Guests enjoy a meal prepared by Michelin Three-Star Chef Michael Tusk. Understated place settings allowed the food and wines to take center stage. Chef Tusk's Porcini Risotto.

Tusk Porcini Risotto

Makes 8 appetizer servings

Michelin Three-Star Chef Michael Tusk of Quince and Cotogna, along with his private events team at Tusk Events in San Francisco, prepared this superb dish for the Huneeus' dinner guests.

PAN-ROASTED PORCINI MUSHROOMS

1½ pounds fresh porcini or wild mushrooms (shiitake, cremini, or portobello)
Olive oil
1 tablespoon fresh thyme leaves

8 tablespoons unsalted butter, cut into pieces
Kosher salt to taste

Brush mushrooms gently to remove any dirt; washing will make many mushrooms soggy. Cut the mushroom caps and stems into larger than bite-size pieces, as they will shrink when they are cooked.

Heat sauté pan over medium-high heat until hot. Add enough olive oil to cover bottom of pan. Sauté mushrooms in olive oil until browned on all sides.

Add thyme and butter. Cook until butter is foamy and lightly browned and mushrooms are tender, stirring frequently. Season with salt and set aside.

RISOTTO

4 cups vegetable or mushroom stock or broth
1 tablespoon unsalted butter
½ small white onion, finely chopped
1 cup arborio rice
1 large pinch of saffron
1 cup white wine

2 cups cold unsalted butter, cut into cubes
½ cup freshly grated Parmigiano-Reggiano cheese
Kosher salt to taste
Pan-Roasted Porcini Mushrooms
Sprigs of fresh thyme
Fresh porcini mushrooms

Warm stock in a saucepan over medium heat.

Melt 1 tablespoon butter in a large saucepan over medium heat. Add onion and cook for 3 minutes or until translucent, stirring frequently. Add rice and saffron and cook until rice is fragrant and looks toasted, stirring constantly. Add wine and cook until alcohol has been cooked off.

Add enough warm stock to partially cover rice mixture. Simmer for 2 to 3 minutes or until stock is absorbed, stirring frequently. Repeat with remaining stock, cooking for a total of 15 to 18 minutes.

Remove rice mixture from heat. Add cold butter cubes a few at a time, stirring to incorporate after each addition. Stir in Parmigiano-Reggiano and salt. (You may need to add a splash or two of stock to the rice to adjust consistency.) Stir in Pan-Roasted Porcini Mushrooms.

Spoon the risotto onto individual plates or onto a serving platter. Garnish with thyme sprigs and freshly shaved porcini mushrooms.

Capture
the Wind

An old Chinese proverb says, "When the winds of change blow, some people build walls; others build windmills." Building a windmill is just what Mike and Sandy Davis did when creating their Calistoga winery in 2011, after retiring from two decades in technology. The concept of capturing the wind is part of the fabric of the Davis Estates brand. The iconic windmill appears on their label and capsule, and even some of their wines such as Zephyr and Pinwheel reference the wind.

One fall evening, three generations of the Davis family and their close friends gathered to celebrate Mike's birthday. It marked a special year, as grandson Chase was there to help Mike blow out his candles. Sandy is a passionate home cook, but given their dynamic lifestyle and her desire to be with her grandson and friends, she asked their winery chef, Mark Caldwell, to prepare some of Mike's favorite dishes using her recipes.

Sandy Davis's Ceviche, Beef Kabobs, and Chocolate Truffle Torte made up the simple and satiating supper. The group ate at a massive redwood table with a remarkable centerpiece of eucalyptus and magnolia leaves, succulents, and roses imbedded in the crevices of gnarly old grapevines. Hammered copper chargers and votive candles accented the earthy arrangement, reflecting Sandy's desire to have the party feel "comfortable with a certain elegance."

As dramatic as the setting indoors was, the expansive vista from the Davis's property took center stage. Mike and Sandy's romance with Napa Valley began more than thirty years ago on a weekend date to wine country. Mike, who spent summers as a child camping in Napa Valley, had wanted to share wine country with Sandy. "Ever since that date," says Mike, "we've had a dream to have a home in Napa someday. We never imagined that we would own a winery."

That night, they drank to realizing a goal, toasting the winds of fortune that had brought them this far and imagining where fate might take Chase to carry on his grandparents' legacy.

Opposite: A snake of ancient grapevines wove its way down the dinner table. Below: Visitors to Davis Estates find a meticulously restored 1922 barn, a modern winery, and an elegant hospitality center with sweeping views of the valley. Tastings require advance reservations.

Menu

Sandy Davis's Ceviche
Halibut, Roma Tomatoes, Green Onions,
Serranos, Avocado, Cilantro, Lime Juice
Reserve Sauvignon Blanc

Beef Kabobs
Davis Family Marinade, Zucchini,
Bell Peppers, Yellow Squash, Onion,
served on Wild Rice
Zephyr Private Reserve Red

Chocolate Truffle Torte
Raspberries, Raspberry Coulis,
Whipped Cream
Pinwheel Cabernet Franc

Sandy Davis's Ceviche

Makes 8 to 12 servings

Serve over a bed of arugula with slices of a crusty baguette. The bright flavors of the ceviche pair well with Davis Estates Sauvignon Blanc.

- 3 pounds finely diced halibut fillets or other firm, mild fish
- 3½ cups fresh lime juice
- 4 cups finely chopped Roma tomatoes
- 5 green onions, thinly sliced
- 4 serrano chiles, seeded and minced
- ½ cup chopped fresh cilantro
- ¼ cup white vinegar
- ¼ cup Davis Estates extra-virgin olive oil
- 1 tablespoon hot sauce
- 1 large avocado, finely diced
- Salt and freshly ground black pepper to taste

Combine fish and lime juice in a large glass or plastic bowl, mixing gently. Cover with plastic wrap and refrigerate for 2 hours or until fish is opaque in the center.

Drain fish, discarding liquid. Stir in tomatoes, green onions, chiles, and cilantro. Combine vinegar, olive oil, and hot sauce in a small bowl and mix well; stir into ceviche mixture. Fold in avocado and add salt and pepper.

Opposite, top: Sandy Davis's Ceviche is a family favorite. Opposite, bottom: A dramatic arrangement of hydrangeas and greens. Clockwise from left: Cheeses were served before dinner. Brandon Davis, his wife, Erica, and their son, Chase, joined the celebration. A breathtaking view was the backdrop to dinner.

Above: Beef Kabobs were served with wild rice. Opposite, clockwise from top: A fifty-foot working windmill adds to the mystique of the estate. Zephyr Reserve Red paired perfectly with the beef. Chef Mark Caldwell cooked a meal designed especially for Mike. The place settings were adorned with eucalyptus.

Beef Kabobs

Makes 8 to 10 servings

3 pounds top sirloin steak, cut into 1½-inch cubes

1 cup Davis Estates extra-virgin olive oil

1 tablespoon grated lemon zest

½ cup fresh lemon juice

16 small garlic cloves, minced

4 medium shallots, minced

4 jalapeño peppers, seeded and finely minced

½ cup chopped fresh oregano

½ cup chopped fresh parsley

20 bamboo skewers

1 red onion, cut into wedges and separated

3 small zucchini, cut into 1-inch slices

3 small yellow summer squash, cut into 1-inch slices

2 large red bell peppers, cut into 1-inch pieces

2 large yellow bell peppers, cut into 1-inch pieces

2 large orange bell peppers, cut into 1-inch pieces

Salt and freshly ground pepper to taste

Place beef in a large resealable plastic bag. Stir olive oil, lemon zest, lemon juice, garlic, shallots, jalapeños, oregano, and parsley in a bowl; pour ⅔ cup marinade over beef, reserving remaining marinade for basting. Seal bag and refrigerate for 3 to 4 hours.

Soak skewers in water for 30 minutes or longer. Preheat grill to medium-high. Drain beef, discarding marinade. Thread beef, onion, zucchini, summer squash, and bell peppers on skewers. Sprinkle with salt and pepper.

Grill kabobs for 10 to 12 minutes or until vegetables are tender and beef reaches desired degree of doneness, turning and basting occasionally with reserved marinade.

Chocolate Truffle Torte

Makes 10 to 12 servings

This recipe comes from our dear friend, Chef John Ash. The rich texture and intense chocolate flavor of our favorite dessert pair well with tangy raspberry sauce.

- ½ cup unsalted butter plus more for pan
- 10 ounces bittersweet chocolate, finely chopped
- 1 tablespoon instant espresso powder
- 8 large eggs, separated
- ½ cup sugar, divided
- ¹⁄₁₆ teaspoon kosher salt
- 2 teaspoons grated orange zest
- Whipped cream
- Fresh raspberries

Preheat oven to 350 degrees. Butter a 9-inch springform pan lightly; cut a circle from parchment or waxed paper and place on bottom of pan.

Melt ½ cup butter in a small saucepan over low heat. Stir in chocolate and espresso powder, whisking until melted. Remove from heat and cool slightly.

Beat egg yolks and ¼ cup sugar in a bowl until light in color. Stir in warm chocolate mixture.

Beat egg whites with an electric mixer fitted with whisk attachment until frothy; beat in salt and orange zest. Add remaining ¼ cup sugar gradually, beating until stiff peaks form. Fold a fourth of egg white mixture into chocolate mixture to lighten. Fold in remaining whites.

Pour batter into prepared pan. Bake for 45 minutes (surface will appear cracked). Cool on a wire rack. May serve at room temperature or chilled. Cut torte into wedges and serve with whipped cream and fresh raspberries.

Above: Dessert was served in front of a roaring fire, accompanied by Pinwheel Cabernet Franc. Hydrangeas added color. Right: Chocolate Truffle Torte with fresh raspberries. Opposite: Mike and Sandy with their vintage 1949 Ford tractor.

Mike and Sandy Davis

In 1989, Mike and Sandy started a company in their Southern California garage to provide IT solutions to businesses. Applied Computer Solutions grew to employ hundreds of people in offices nationwide, serving startups to Fortune 500 enterprises. Ready to "retire" in 2010, they sold their interest in the business and turned to Napa Valley to start a new career. One year later, they acquired land and began the redevelopment of a historic vineyard property to create Davis Estates. The couple splits their time between Southern California and wine country.

"I love the dynamic of designing the guest list, menu, and décor for a fun evening. Nothing gives me more pleasure than gathering people that matter together and creating food that speaks to them in a relaxing, comfortable atmosphere." —SANDY DAVIS

A Daring Theatrical Experience

Stepping into a surrealist environment, guests at Raymond Vineyards are transported to a world unlike any other in Napa Valley. Here, the experience goes beyond wine tasting. The opulent tasting salons are adorned with unexpected objects, like crystal chandeliers, leopard print carpets, red velvet, disco balls, and mannequins.

One winter evening, guests joined proprietor Jean-Charles Boisset in the winery's lavish, exclusive Red Room for supper. "Parties should be a magical dreamland for guests, where all their senses are awakened," says Jean-Charles. To accomplish this, he set a massive black lacquer table with a ribbon of red rose petals running down the center, accented by Baccarat crystal butterflies and candlesticks, Ralph Lauren leopard-print chargers, and Christofle silver. Every element was luxurious, especially the jeweled brooches placed at each setting—each brooch uniquely designed by Jean-Charles. Under a red velvet canopy, a massive crystal chandelier illuminated the room, accentuating the decadence.

At the start of the evening, Jean-Charles, known to many as JCB, asked guests to surrender their phones and place them in envelopes with their names on them. He wanted them to experience all aspects of the party. "Today, people look at the world through a little screen," he says. "They need to see, hear, smell, feel, and taste what is around them." He hired a photographer to capture the festivities and share images so that guests would go home with lasting memories.

JCB sparkling wine, Jean-Claude Boisset Chardonnay, and Raymond Cabernet Sauvignon flowed freely. Dinner was a multicourse extravaganza, beginning with foie gras and ending with a tower of French macarons. Jean-Charles raised his hands, summoning guests to do the same, and led them in singing "Le Ban Bourguignon," transporting them to La Paulée in his hometown of Vougeot, France.

When he entertains, Jean-Charles wants his guests to feel curious, daring, and enlightened, giving them the opportunity to discover the unseen. With characteristic flair, Jean-Charles created a memorable theatrical experience for his guests, leaving them feeling as if they had been part of one of the greatest acts of all time.

Below: An eclectic display of picture frames at Raymond Vineyards invites visitors to add their own visage to a work of art. The winery offers unique tasting experiences, including "Winemaker for a Day," where guests blend their own wine. Opposite: Drama unfolded on this opulent table set for an unforgettable dinner.

Jean-Charles Boisset

Born in Burgundy, France, the epicenter of pinot noir and chardonnay, Jean-Charles grew up in the wine world. This showman and entrepreneur moved to California in the early nineties to gain a better understanding of the US market and to expand his family's Boisset Collection. The business now includes more than twenty-five wineries in France and California, including Raymond Vineyards, which was purchased in 2009. Inspired by his family's heritage, Jean-Charles is passionate about both history and innovation, focused on producing terroir-driven wines with a commitment to organic and Biodynamic® farming.

"The pleasure of life is to passionately welcome others into our world and transport them into a journey of imagination and dreams that goes beyond their own personal experiences."

—JEAN-CHARLES BOISSET

Clockwise from left: LVE: Legend Vineyard Exclusive Cabernet Sauvignon is produced in collaboration with singer-songwriter John Legend. The Red Room is designed to make guests feel like they are immersed in a glass of red wine. Cabernet sauvignon was served at a bar surrounded by eclectic objects, including a collection of *Playboy* magazines and a roulette wheel.

How to Create an Opulent and Unforgettable Party

For Jean-Charles Boisset, the success of a great party is when guests are "taken on an enchanted dream where all their senses are awakened and the magic of the moment allows them to escape and discover the unseen." He strives to create a theatrical experience where they feel curious, daring, and enlightened—hoping that they will "visualize life beyond conscious rational control and feel that nothing is impossible."

Every party Jean-Charles hosts is a dramatic production that involves a script, actors, costumes, props, staging, music, and food, intertwined in a way that evokes a powerful emotional response. Here are the steps Boisset takes when working to make a party truly transcendent.

WRITE A SCRIPT
Define the visual and sensory experience guests will have. Think about how the party will arouse the senses of sight, sound, touch, smell, and taste. With this clear vision articulated in a script, work to develop each element.

DEFINE THE AUDIENCE
Create a guest list. In building the audience, think about who will enjoy the production, and assemble a diverse group of people to spice things up.

ORCHESTRATE UNFORGETTABLE MUSIC
Melodies may be live or recorded, in the background providing ambiance, revved up for dancing, or an interlude at a party. Whatever the role of music is, make sure it is noticeable, memorable, and supports the script.

PROVIDE JAW-DROPPING ENTERTAINMENT
A party that is theatrical goes beyond music. Jean-Charles isn't afraid to go over the top. Entertainment can be as simple as sabering a bottle of bubbles or as elaborate as creating a casino environment for gambling or staging a performance in the spirit of Cirque du Soleil. Waiters can be dressed to play a part, and actors or models dressed to theme can add to the experience. Whatever the entertainment, make it irresistible.

SET THE STAGE
Or, in most cases, set the table. Silverware, plates, candles, flowers, napkins, place cards, and menus are all part of the performance. Let the wonderful details of the table awaken the senses and immerse guests in the experience. Be clever, not contrived.

COOK LAVISH FOOD
Each morsel served should arouse not only the mouth but the eyes and nose. Include an amuse-bouche—which, literally translated, means "entertain the mouth"—in the menu. Be daring: serve dishes that push the envelope, like escargots, frog legs, or octopus.

POUR REMARKABLE WINES
In Napa Valley, what is in the glass is often the focal point of a party, and the wines often dictate what dishes are prepared to accompany them. The act of serving wines and talking about them is a big part of the production. On a larger stage, where wine may not be the focus, create a dramatic bar, showcase a signature cocktail, and include the bartenders in the performance.

From top: A stunning Baccarat decanter added to the allure of the table. The label for JCB Passion red blend describes it as "opulent, alluring, and sensual." Opposite: The stage was set for a dramatic dinner party with intriguing details, such as a Lalique Tianlong dragon decanter filled with rose petals and whimsical Bernardaud Banality service plates by Jeff Koons. Both are available from the JCB Tasting Salon in Yountville.

JCB's Indulgent Dinner Menu

Amuse-Bouche
Foie gras sur brioche
Smoked salmon with
lemon on blinis
Beluga caviar on an ivory spoon
Tomato juice façon michou
Cold lobster en papillote
*JCB No. 50 Blanc de Blanc,
Burgundy*

Brittany Oysters and Sea Urchins
*JCB No. 16 White Bordeaux
Blend, Napa Valley*

Cold White Asparagus
Caviar and lemon
*JCB No. 33 Chardonnay, Russian
River Valley, Sonoma*

Comte and Beaufort Soufflé
*Jean-Claude Boisset Corton
Charlemagne, Burgundy*

Blue Lobster
Cooked on seaweed
*Domaine de la Vougeraie Batard
Montrachet, Burgundy*

Quails with Grapes
Pinot noir sauce, ceps, morilles,
butter peas
*JCB No. 3 Pinot Noir,
Russian River Valley /
Burgundy
Jean-Claude Boisset
Clos de la Roche
Côtes de Nuits*

Assorted Cheeses
Langres cheese vol-au-vents
Sheep cheese assortment
Abbaye de Cîteaux de
Bourgogne
Délice de Pommard
*JCB No. 11 Pinot Noir,
Sonoma Coast
JCB No. 1 Cabernet Sauvignon,
Napa Valley*

Dessert Selections
Charlotte à la Framboise
Exotic fruit sorbet
*JCB The Surrealist Red Wine,
Napa Valley*

Above: An enticing selection of cheese and charcuterie from Atelier Fine Foods in Yountville.

Opposite: Jean-Charles Boisset and James Ayers work to select the perfect cheeses for an event.

Marrying Two Culinary Obsessions: Wine and Cheese

Like wine, cheese is a precious commodity. Both provide a connection to the land, are labor-intensive products, and owe their existence to extremely dedicated, often obsessive individuals focused on perfecting their craft. This may explain why those passionate about wine are often equally taken by cheese and why marrying the two has become an art.

James Ayers, Chief Gourmand and Cheesemonger at Atelier Fine Foods in Yountville, is a master at pairing cheese (and charcuterie) with wine. With an extensive selection of cheeses to pull from, he works to create the perfect experience that shows the purity of cheese and the escalation of texture and smell with very intense visual elements.

Some recommended cheeses for popular wines are:

SPARKLING WINE
Brillat-Savarin: A triple-cream cheese that is rich and intense. Made from pasteurized cow's milk on the Îls-de-France, it is named after nineteenth-century gastronome and epicure, Jean Anthelme Brillat-Savarin.

SAUVIGNON BLANC
Humboldt Fog: This iconic American goat cheese is mild, smooth, and dense.

CHARDONNAY
Abbaye de Cîteaux: From the Cîteaux Abbey located in Burgundy, France, and made by monks, this cheese has an earthy, creamy, and milky taste.

Bellwether Farms' San Andreas: Naturally oily and deliciously fatty, this cheese works with an oaky and buttery California chardonnay.

PINOT NOIR
Ami du Chambertin: A soft French artisan cow's milk cheese produced in the Gevrey-Chambertin region of Burgundy. It is aromatic and extremely long lasting.

Langres: A semisoft cow's milk cheese from France that is Boisset's grandmother's favorite. It melts in the mouth, leaving a complex taste that is pure and elegant.

CABERNET SAUVIGNON
Comté: A French cheese made from cow's milk. Best when aged thirty-six months, it is dense and nutty with a buttery texture. A more readily available cheese might be Gruyère or a dry asiago.

Parmigiano-Reggiano: When aged, this is a nutty, nuanced hard cheese that is salty and rich.

Delicate and Enticing Foie Gras

To add a bit of French flair to a dinner party, consider serving foie gras, a popular and well-known delicacy. A recurring addition to the menu when dining with Jean-Charles, foie gras is a luxurious rich dish made from duck liver, considered by gourmands to be one of life's greatest pleasures.

Typically found prepared in the form of a terrine or torchon, foie gras is served at room temperature as a starter course with triangles of brioche bread, jam or fruit compote, and a sprinkling of sea salt.

The more decadent way to prepare it is to slice a lobe of foie gras into medallions and quickly sear it in a hot dry skillet, serving it with a port or balsamic reduction or a warm fig or apple compote. Pour a glass of sparkling wine or pinot noir to accompany the decadence.

Vinum, Cantus, Amor

The bell that appears on the Ceja Vineyards label rings to the Ceja family's passions. Around the rim are the words *vinum, cantus, amor*—Latin for wine, song, love. In addition to the words, the bell itself is symbolic: a reminder of the family's longtime dream to build a Mission-inspired winery since acquiring the Carneros vineyard property in 1983.

One Friday evening, the extended family came to Casa Ceja for a fiesta to celebrate the start of harvest. Pinot noir and chardonnay grapes were ready to be picked, and it was time to enjoy a meal together, give thanks, and celebrate their accomplishments. The children of grape pickers, proprietors Pedro, Amelia, Armando, and Martha all came to Napa from Mexico when they were very young. Today, these college-educated Mexican-Americans are living a lifelong dream.

Amelia, who believes that food is at the heart of everything, learned to cook from her grandmother and then passed the tradition on to her children. That evening, three generations of Ceja women—Amelia; her mother-in-law, Mamá Juanita; and her daughter, Dalia—prepared traditional Mexican dishes that would sing with Ceja's wines. Educating people on how to serve wine with world cuisine is one of Amelia's many passions. On the menu was Sea Bass Ceviche, paired with chardonnay, and Chuletas de Cordero (lamb lollypops) with cilantro-infused rice, paired with pinot noir.

Setting a festive table, Dalia mixed contemporary and traditional elements. She selected a shimmery modern tablecloth in burnt orange and used gold chargers to play off the colors in classic Mexican ceramic plates. Paying homage to their heritage, she placed two traditional Catrina figurines on the table to honor their ancestors.

Frequent family gatherings are important to the Cejas. They often remark that it takes a talented family, working together, to consistently grow the best grapes and produce the most balanced wines. It is a legacy they cherish and hope to inspire for the next generation. After all, says Amelia, "This is what life is all about—sitting down to eat with your family over good food and great wine."

Opposite: Amelia Ceja puts the final touches on her colorful ceviche. Below: A capilla (chapel) on the Ceja's Napa Carneros estate speaks to the Mission-inspired winery they will soon construct. The Cejas welcome visitors for tastings at their Sonoma tasting room on Highway 12, and, once complete, at their new Napa winery.

Sea Bass Ceviche

Makes 6 servings

2 pounds boneless, skinless sea bass steaks
2 cups fresh lime juice
1 (1-inch) piece fresh ginger, finely grated
½ teaspoon salt
1 teaspoon freshly ground white pepper
½ Manzano or other spicy pepper, seeded and minced
1 jalapeño pepper, seeded and minced

½ red onion, diced
2 Roma tomatoes, seeded and diced
3 tablespoons vinegar from jarred pickled jalapeño peppers
1 teaspoon dried oregano
3 tablespoons olive oil
½ cup chopped fresh cilantro
1 avocado, diced

Cut fish into bite-size pieces. Combine fish, lime juice, ginger, salt, and white pepper in a large glass bowl and mix well. Cover and refrigerate for 1 hour; stir.

Drain and discard ⅔ of liquid. Add Manzano, jalapeño, onion, tomatoes, jalapeño vinegar, and oregano and mix well. Stir in olive oil. Cover and let stand for 15 minutes or until mixture reaches room temperature. Stir in cilantro and adjust salt to taste. Spoon mixture into margarita glasses and garnish with avocado and additional cilantro. Serve with corn tostaditas, tortilla chips, or endive.

Menu

Sea Bass Ceviche
Garnished with diced avocado and cilantro
Napa Valley Carneros Chardonnay

Chuletas de Cordero with Chimichurri
Cilantro-infused rice
Carneros Pinot Noir

Almond Flan
Stone Fruit Salsa
Dulce Beso Late Harvest Wine

Amelia and Dalia Ceja

Recognized as "Woman of the Year" in 2005 by the California legislature for "breaking the glass ceiling in a very competitive business," Amelia runs Ceja's day-to-day operations. She is the first Mexican-American woman to be elected president of a winery. Dalia, who has an MBA in wine marketing, was named "Woman of the Year" by the Napa Valley Hispanic Chamber of Commerce in 2011.

Opposite: Dalia pours pinot noir to accompany the Chuletas de Cordero (lamb lollypops). Ceja's chardonnay was the perfect pairing for Sea Bass Ceviche. Left: The festive table included stunning handmade Talavera ceramic plates that the Cejas brought home from Mexico.

Feast of the Seasons

Meadowood Napa Valley is the region's epicenter of wine and cuisine. Tucked in a tranquil canyon, this secluded Relais & Châteaux resort is the ideal location for a wine country retreat ... and the perfect venue for all occasions, from casual gatherings to lifetime celebrations. Many locals and visitors turn to Meadowood to help them realize their vision for an exclusive, unforgettable event.

Cuisine in Napa Valley revolves around locally grown fresh ingredients, and Meadowood Napa Valley is no exception. "Each season, the garden brings something new to the kitchen and to our events," says Patrick Davila, director at the resort. Patrick trusts Meadowood's Estate Chef Alejandro Ayala to weave seasonal ingredients like spring peas, summer melons, fall beets, or winter greens into his menus. Chef Ayala visits the Meadowood garden each morning for inspiration, looking for unexpected ingredients to boost flavor and add layers of complexity. A summer salad, for example, may get a fresh update with heirloom tomato gelée, pickled melons, burrata air, and basil dust. Dehydrated beets and pistachios might form a crunchy "soil" base for a fall salad. The use of seasonal ingredients extends to Meadowood's craft cocktails. Master mixologist Scott Beattie brings garden produce to his drinks by adding lemon verbena to an Aperol Sour or fresh cucumbers to a Vodka Collins.

Patrick is an expert host whose team plans intimate events for Napa Valley's most discerning hosts—at Meadowood, in homes and wineries, and nationwide through Estate Events by Meadowood, which provides an intimate, exceptional Napa Valley culinary experience. He has sage advice for every host and hostess. "Entertaining begins with preparation," he says, "and is most memorable in its presentation. The details play out in flawless execution." To create an exquisite presentation, Patrick suggests looking at how each place is set—creating a unique centerpiece, carefully arranging the ingredients on each beautiful plate, and adding an element of discovery and surprise. The final touch is the execution. Personalized tableside service and a well-laid plan produces a memorable experience, leaving no detail to chance.

Below: The Restaurant at Meadowood, The Grill at Meadowood, and gorgeous event spaces are housed in the timeless Club House. Opposite: A professionally maintained lawn is the site of many friendly games of croquet, which are part of numerous celebrations.

Aperol Sour

Makes 1 serving

- 1 ounce (2 tablespoons) Distillery 209 gin
- 1 ounce (2 tablespoons) Aperol or Campari
- 2 tablespoons fresh lemon juice
- 2 teaspoons simple syrup
- 2 tablespoons chilled club soda
  Orange slices, lemon slices, lemon verbena, edible flowers

Combine gin, Aperol, lemon juice, and simple syrup in an ice-filled cocktail shaker. Shake vigorously. Strain cocktail into an ice-filled rocks glass. Add club soda and stir. Garnish with fruit slices, herbs, and flowers.

Chilled Spring Cauliflower Soup

Makes 8 to 10 servings

Cauliflower Garnishes	2 heads cauliflower, chopped
1 tablespoon olive oil	1 cup crème fraîche
2 tablespoons butter	Kosher salt to taste
1 celery stalk, chopped	Milk, optional
1 large leek, chopped	Celery leaves
4 cups milk	2 tablespoons toasted hazelnuts, chopped
2 cups water	Edible flowers

Prepare Cauliflower Garnishes, if desired. Cover and chill until ready to serve.

Heat olive oil and butter in a large saucepan over medium-low heat. Add celery stalk and leek. Cook for 5 minutes or until tender but not browned. Stir in milk, water, and chopped cauliflower. Cook over medium heat for 45 minutes or until cauliflower is tender, stirring occasionally. Remove from heat and purée with an immersion blender or transfer to a blender and purée, in batches, until smooth. Cover and chill. Fold in crème fraîche and add salt. Stir in milk if mixture is too thick.

Arrange Cauliflower Garnishes, celery leaves, and hazelnuts in a circle inside serving bowls. Pour soup tableside, beginning in center and then around outside of circle. Garnish with edible flowers.

CAULIFLOWER GARNISHES

1 small head cauliflower	1 bay leaf
½ cup sherry	1 tablespoon Espelette or other ground
½ cup white wine vinegar	chili powder
¼ cup sugar	1 tablespoon olive oil
6 whole black peppercorns	

Cut cauliflower into small florets and divide into thirds. Combine sherry, vinegar, sugar, peppercorns, and bay leaf in a small saucepan and bring to a boil. Remove from heat and add a third of the florets to pickling liquid. Cover and refrigerate for 6 to 12 hours; drain. Cook a third of the florets in boiling water for 3 minutes or until al dente. Plunge immediately into ice water to stop the cooking process; drain. Sprinkle lightly with Espelette; cover and chill until ready to serve. Heat olive oil in a skillet over medium-high heat. Add the remaining cauliflower and cook for 5 to 7 minutes or until golden brown, stirring frequently. Cover and chill until ready to serve.

Opposite: Chilled Spring Cauliflower Soup with hazelnuts and garden flowers. Above: Surrounded by moss, ancient grapevines made a dramatic centerpiece for an early spring luncheon.

"Entertaining is the art of facilitating surprise, comfort, enjoyment, and discovery for your guests—all the while making each carefully curated detail feel like the most natural thing in the world." —PATRICK DAVILA

Summer Spoons

Makes 4 dozen

½ cup champagne vinegar
½ cup white wine vinegar
¼ cup sugar
6 whole black peppercorns
½ honeydew melon, peeled and seeded
½ cantaloupe, peeled and seeded
2 pounds ripe heirloom tomatoes
2 gelatin sheets (silver strength)

1 cup cold water, divided
1 tablespoon unflavored powdered gelatin
  Flaky sea salt to taste
1 large bunch fresh basil
¼ cup fresh basil leaves
1 (4-ounce) ball burrata cheese
¼ cup whipping cream

Combine vinegars, sugar, and peppercorns in a small saucepan over medium-high heat. Bring to a boil and remove from heat. Cool to room temperature. Scoop honeydew melon and cantaloupe into 4 dozen small balls each with a parisienne scoop or ¼- to ½-inch melon baller. Stir into vinegar mixture. Cover and chill for 2 to 12 hours, stirring occasionally.

Core tomatoes and cut an "X" in each base. Blanch tomatoes in boiling water for 30 seconds. Plunge immediately into ice water to stop the cooking process. Peel and quarter tomatoes. Place tomatoes and any liquid, in batches, in a blender or food processor. Blend until smooth. Strain mixture through a cheesecloth-lined colander, discarding solids. Measure and reserve 2 cups, saving any remaining juice for other uses. Cover and chill until ready to assemble.

Soften gelatin sheets in ½ cup cold water in a shallow bowl. Let stand until softened. Combine powdered gelatin and remaining ½ cup cold water in a small bowl. Let stand for 1 minute. Heat reserved tomato juice in a saucepan over medium-low heat. Drain gelatin sheets, discarding water. Stir into tomato juice. Stir powdered gelatin mixture into tomato juice. Cook for 2 minutes or until gelatin dissolves, stirring gently. Stir in salt. Pour mixture into a 9-inch square dish. Cover and chill until firm.

Preheat oven to 140 degrees. Wash large bunch of basil and pat dry, removing stems. Arrange basil on a parchment-lined baking sheet and bake for 2 to 4 hours or until dried and crumbly. Cool completely and grind to a powder in a spice mill.

Cut tomato gelatin into ½-inch cubes. Drain melon. Chiffonade or thinly slice ¼ cup basil. Cut burrata into small pieces and combine with cream in a 2-cup glass measuring cup. Process with an immersion blender until light and fluffy.

To serve, place 3 tomato gelatin cubes, 1 honeydew ball, and 1 cantaloupe ball in each serving spoon. Top with basil chiffonade and flaky sea salt. Place about ½ teaspoon whipped burrata on each spoon and sprinkle with ground basil.

Cucumber Collins

Makes 1 serving

1½ ounces (3 tablespoons) Square One cucumber vodka
1 tablespoon fresh lemon juice
1 tablespoon simple syrup
1½ teaspoons yuzu juice or fresh lemon juice
2–4 tablespoons chilled club soda
  Cucumber slices
  Edible flowers

Combine vodka, lemon juice, simple syrup, and yuzu juice in an ice-filled cocktail shaker. Shake vigorously. Strain cocktail into an ice-filled Collins glass. Add club soda and stir. Garnish with cucumber slices and edible flowers.

Opposite: Wire mesh and hydrangeas added texture and interest to the Summer Spoons presentation.
Left: Estate chef Alejandro Ayala is a twenty-seven-year veteran of the Meadowood kitchen and a James Beard Award Honoree.

Bourbon Buck

Makes 1 serving

- 1½ ounces (3 tablespoons) Woodford Reserve bourbon
- 1 tablespoon Shrub and Co. Honey Wildflower Shrub
- 1 tablespoon fresh lemon juice
- 2 dashes Angostura bitters
- ½ cup Bundaberg or other ginger beer
- Freshly grated nutmeg

Combine bourbon, shrub, lemon juice, and bitters in an ice-filled cocktail shaker. Shake vigorously. Strain cocktail into an ice-filled copper mug. Add ginger beer and stir. Sprinkle with grated nutmeg.

Right: A "Welcome to the World" baby shower. Opposite, clockwise from top: Fall pumpkins in the Meadowood garden. Events Director Alex Hernandez collaborates with a host. Beet chips and pistachios were the base for the salad.

Fall Beet Salad

Makes 8 servings

- 16 baby Chioggia or red beets
- 16 baby golden beets
- 1 cup plus 2 tablespoons extra-virgin olive oil, divided
- 4 large red beets, rinsed, peeled and quartered
- ¼ cup water
- Flaky sea salt to taste
- 3 tablespoons roasted and salted pistachios, finely chopped
- 3 seedless oranges, divided
- ¼ cup champagne vinegar
- 4 ounces goat cheese
- 3 cups mixed baby lettuces

Preheat oven to 350 degrees. Cut leaves from baby beets, leaving long tap roots. Toss beets in 1 tablespoon olive oil and place in a baking dish. Add ½-inch of water and cover tightly with aluminum foil. Bake for 45 minutes or until tender. Drain and let stand until cool enough to handle. Remove skin, keeping root intact. Set aside.

Reduce oven temperature to 275 degrees. Place large red beets and ¼ cup water in a blender and blend until smooth. Place a fine mesh strainer over a large bowl and pour beet mixture through the strainer, pressing with spatula to remove all juice from pulp. Save juice for other uses. Combine beet pulp and 1 tablespoon olive oil. Add salt. Spread pulp on a parchment-lined baking sheet and bake for 2 hours or until dry and crispy (use a dehydrator or convection oven for faster results). Cool completely and chop. Stir in pistachios.

Squeeze juice from 1 orange into a small bowl. Whisk in vinegar and remaining 1 cup olive oil. Add salt. Shape goat cheese into 8 quenelles or small cylinders. Cut remaining oranges into segments.

Create a circle of the beet mixture in the center of serving plates using a ring mold. Arrange reserved baby beets, root side up, goat cheese quenelles, and orange segments in a circle around beet mixture. Top with baby lettuces and drizzle each with orange vinaigrette.

Winter Lobster Salad

Makes 8 servings

½ cup champagne vinegar
½ cup white wine vinegar
¼ cup sugar
6 whole black peppercorns
2 small Granny Smith apples, peeled
2 celery stalks, diced ⅛ inch thick
4 (1¼-pound) Maine lobsters
2 tablespoons mayonnaise
1–2 teaspoons fresh lemon zest

¼ cup fresh lemon juice
Flaky sea salt to taste
1 cup green grapes
¼ cup crème fraîche
¼ cup toasted pecans, very finely chopped
Extra-virgin olive oil
3 finger limes, optional
½ cup micro celery or celery leaves
Edible flowers

Combine vinegars, sugar, and peppercorns in a small saucepan over medium-high heat. Bring to a boil. Remove from heat and cool to room temperature. Scoop apples into balls with a parisienne scoop or very small melon baller. Add apples and celery stalks to vinegar mixture. Cover and chill for 2 to 12 hours. (Remove peppercorns before serving.)

Steam lobsters or cook in boiling salted water to cover for 10 to 12 minutes. Plunge immediately into ice water. Remove shells from tails and cut meat into bite-size pieces; set aside. Remove shells from claws and place meat in a small bowl. Stir in mayonnaise, lemon zest, lemon juice, and salt.

Arrange lobster tail meat and claw meat mixture evenly on salad plates and top evenly with grapes. Dollop crème fraîche around salad. Top lobster with apple mixture using a slotted spoon. Sprinkle pecans evenly around salad. Drizzle salad with extra-virgin olive oil and salt. Slice finger limes and squeeze citrus "caviar" evenly over salad. Garnish with micro celery and edible flowers.

Jamaican Sorrel

Makes 6 cups

5   cups water
5   teaspoons dried hibiscus flowers
1   (2-inch) piece fresh ginger, peeled and sliced
2   teaspoons whole allspice
½   teaspoon cracked or ground allspice
½   teaspoon whole cloves
2   cups sugar

Combine water, hibiscus, ginger, whole allspice, cracked allspice, and cloves in a saucepan over medium-high heat. Bring mixture to a boil. Remove from heat. Cover and steep for 12 hours. Strain mixture, returning a few whole allspice to mixture. Add sugar, stirring until dissolved. Cover and chill for up to 2 weeks.

Right: Celery greens and edible flowers added color to a delicate lobster salad.

Opposite: A manzanita branch made a dramatic presentation for arancini. Votive candles were set on stumps of varying heights for a fireside dinner.

Paella Arancini

Makes 4 dozen

1 pound fresh mussels	Kosher salt and freshly ground pepper
2 tablespoons extra-virgin olive oil	to taste
2 tablespoons finely chopped white onion	1 tablespoon chopped fresh thyme
2 cups arborio rice	1 tablespoon chopped fresh parsley
1 cup white wine	1 cup all-purpose flour
½ to 1 teaspoon saffron threads	3 eggs
3 cups chicken stock or broth	2 cups panko breadcrumbs
½ cup finely diced smoked Spanish chorizo	Vegetable oil for frying
3 tablespoons butter	Pimentón Aïoli
1 cup (4 ounces) freshly grated Parmesan	Thinly sliced Spanish chorizo
cheese	Micro cilantro leaves

Rinse mussels under cold running water while scrubbing with a vegetable brush, discarding any with broken shells. Steam mussels for 5 minutes or until shells open, discarding any that do not open. Remove mussel meat from shells and set meat aside.

Heat olive oil in a medium pot or saucepan over low heat. Add onion and cook for 2 to 3 minutes or until translucent. Increase heat and stir in rice and wine. Cook until wine evaporates, stirring constantly. Stir in saffron and a third of the chicken stock. Continue to cook and add remaining stock until rice is tender and liquid is absorbed, stirring constantly. Stir in reserved mussel meat, diced chorizo, butter, and Parmesan. Add salt and pepper. Remove from heat and stir in thyme and parsley; let cool to room temperature.

Place flour in a shallow bowl. Whisk eggs in a shallow bowl. Place panko in a shallow bowl. Roll rice mixture into 1- to 1½-inch balls. Roll in flour and dip in eggs, letting excess drain back into bowl. Roll in panko and set aside.

Heat ½ to 1 inch of oil in a large cast-iron skillet to 350 degrees. Add balls in batches and cook for 5 minutes or until crisp and golden brown, turning occasionally. Drain on paper towels. Spoon a drop of Pimentón Aïoli onto each arancini and top each with one slice of chorizo and a micro cilantro leaf.

PIMENTÓN AÏOLI

2 egg yolks	2-3 teaspoons smoked paprika
2 tablespoons fresh lemon juice	1 cup extra-virgin olive oil
1 teaspoon ground coriander	Kosher salt to taste

Combine eggs, lemon juice, coriander, and paprika in a food processor. Add olive oil in a slow stream until mixture is thickened, processing constantly and stopping to scrape side of processor with a spatula, if necessary. Add salt. Cover and chill until ready to serve. Makes 1¼ cups.

Adding Drama to the Table

Every event begins with the setting. Layering elements to create personal style and the desired tone for an occasion is an art. Lindsey Rion, owner of Rion Designs, knows how to turn a blank canvas or an artfully decorated space into a visual masterpiece. Here, she shares insight on how she orchestrates some of Napa Valley's most exquisite events.

For dinner parties, the surrounding itself sets the tone. "Get creative with what you have," says Lindsey. "Look around your home and be authentic to the space." First, look to the table. The natural patina of wood grain or a table cloaked in rawhide can be as elegant as a white table linen.

Next, use the landscape of the table and juxtaposition of soft and hard materials to create allure. "The mixed textures of a tablescape keeps things interesting. For example, try the combination of wood and metal, linen with raw rope, or leather and lace," says Lindsey.

Lindsey also encourages connecting the décor to the purpose of the party. When layering decorative accessories and individual place settings, punctuate the design with a hint of the unexpected. "The natural bounty of Napa Valley creates irresistible elements to augment any table design. Pair those with pieces that are unique to the evening," she says. If it is a musical affair, scatter the setting with guitar picks. If it's a formal event, set off glass stemware with opulent candlesticks and black and white accents.

The table opposite uses a black wood table as the first layer of design. The soft drape of the fabric table runner, interspersed with mixed florals in vases of various height and texture, pair with crystalline quartz and antlers to add interest.

"Dare to introduce authentic elements and layer colors and textures. The nuances of the design and an eclectic mix of curated pieces add personality and visual interest to any setting." —LINDSEY RION

Look to the West

On Pritchard Hill, often called Napa's "Rodeo Drive," there is a building that looks more like a horse barn or a structure from an old mining town than one of the Valley's toniest wineries. Within this rustic building is BRAND Napa Valley—a state-of-the-art winery with stunning caves, breathtaking views, and an inviting lounge for wine tasting. BRAND's unpretentious exterior and magnificent interior could also describe a bottle of its highly coveted mountain-grown cabernet sauvignon.

The views of Lake Hennessey and Mount St. Helena drew owners Ed and Deb Fitts to this spectacular property in 2006. Since then, they have taken great care in developing BRAND Napa Valley. Each step in the endeavor was deliberate—from hiring the right experts to create their vineyard to the double horseshoes embossed on their wine label to celebrate their beloved Missouri Fox Trotters. "This land is ripe with promise," says Ed. "We are on the journey of a lifetime."

One cool August evening, Ed and Deb hosted dear friends for dinner on their terrace. This intimate and simple gathering was typical for the Fitts; they eat outside almost every summer night, watching the sun drop behind the mountains. Deb set an understated table with beautiful neutral ecru linens and white china, letting the vista take the stage. A bouquet of zinnias from the garden brought a pop of color to the table, as did a cardoon and olive branch resting on each napkin. Given the chill in the air, she placed a wool wrap on each lady's chair, and Ed built a fire in the outdoor fireplace. Supper was equally elegant and simple, with Deb cooking one of her favorite recipes—Chilean Sea Bass with Miso Maple Glaze with glazed carrots to complement the wines.

As the lyrics from an iconic rock song state, "There's a feeling you get when you look to the west." It's clear that Ed and Deb were influenced by the ruggedness and beauty of the West when developing their winery. Gazing west at the lake and the valley, their friends felt that time could stand still.

Below: BRAND welcomes serious wine enthusiasts and collectors by appointment only. Its wines are available almost exclusively through a mailing list. Opposite: A sophisticated yet understated table allowed the sunset over Lake Hennessey to be the star.

Menu

Onion Marmalade Tartlet
Caramelized Figs and Nueske Bacon

Chilean Sea Bass with Miso Maple Glaze
Sweet Potatoes with Coconut Yams and
Glazed Carrots

Artisan Cheese Selection
L'Amuse, Midnight Moon, Toma,
Warm Gougères, Black Pepper Shortbread,
and Savory Meringue
Almonds, Smoked Honey, and Savory Granola

Seasonal Petits Fours
Meyer Lemon Poppy Seed
Strawberry Pâte de Fruit

BRAND Napa Valley Wines

Chilean Sea Bass with Miso Maple Glaze

Makes 6 servings

This light and flavorful dish is a favorite of Deb's because it is healthy and cooks fast—so she doesn't have to spend a lot of time in the kitchen. Also because there are a lot of variations one can make to change up the flavors. Deb's favorite variations are serving the fish with glazed carrots, mashed white sweet potatoes, or in a bowl with a little miso soup/broth.

½ cup dark miso paste
½ cup maple syrup
1 tablespoon low-sodium soy sauce or
tamari sauce

6 (6-ounce) Chilean sea bass or black cod
fillets (skin-on or skinless)
2 tablespoons canola oil or olive oil

Whisk miso, maple syrup, and soy sauce in a small bowl. Spread mixture over both sides of fish in a dish. Cover and refrigerate for 6 hours or overnight.

Preheat oven to 350 degrees. Remove fish from marinade, draining off excess marinade.

Heat the canola oil in a large cast-iron or ovenproof skillet over medium-high heat. Sear fillets, skin side down, for 1 minute. Turn fillets over. Transfer skillet to oven and bake for 5 to 8 minutes or just until fish is cooked through and opaque in the center.

Above: An artful plate with glazed carrots and sea bass. Left: BRAND's highly coveted cabernet sauvignon. Opposite, from top: The table setting was simple—from elegant flowers to natural linens.

The Fitts with their Missouri Foxtrotters (left to right): Maggie Mae, Rascal, Gracie, and Gypsy.

Ed and Deb Fitts

The founder and CEO of a Pennsylvania-based paper company, Ed Fitts sold his business and retired in 2004. Two years later, he was a homeowner in Napa with a small block of vineyard. Realizing the stature of his terroir, he and his wife, Deb, set out to create a wine brand. Today, BRAND is regarded as one of Napa's most highly coveted "cult" wines.

Riches of Regusci Ranch

Nestled below the towering Palisades in the heart of the Stags Leap District is one of Napa Valley's historic properties. Built in 1878 and purchased by the Regusci family in 1932, the 286-acre Regusci Ranch has evolved from one of Napa's earliest wineries, to a dairy farm, to a working cattle ranch, and back to a world-class winery. To relax on the tasting room terrace and take in views of the valley while sipping Regusci's estate wines is an unforgettable experience. The Reguscis want every guest to feel at home—like they are part of the family.

The two-acre estate garden was the site for a summer dinner party with proprietors Jim and Laura Regusci. Set under a whimsical canopy, the dinner table reflected the garden: zinnias, sunflowers, and herbs were part of the centerpiece, and leather pruning shear holsters held the flatware. Laura used four wine barrels, one set at the base of each canopy pole, to provide service for hors d'oeuvres, wine, and water.

That evening, Jim and Laura shared the unique history of the land and introduced guests to their chickens, rooster, turkeys, hogs, goats, horses, and peacock. The guests strolled through the olive and citrus groves and a tunnel of broom corn to arrive at the dinner table. Supper was cooked from as many ingredients from the ranch as possible. The focal points of the meal were the freshly harvested produce and the heritage pork tenderloin raised on the ranch. "We care deeply about farming, the sustainability of food production, and protecting the land," says Laura. "To us, it is simply the right thing to do—in part because it's what Jim's family has done forever." The fourth generation of Reguscis embrace their family's heritage and are dedicated to preserving the health and vitality of the land.

Jim and Laura's friends lingered well into the night around the firepit, where dessert was served. Cuddled under warm blankets, they roasted giant marshmallows, dipping them in chocolate bourbon sauce, and sipped estate cabernet. It was the perfect ending to a rich evening on the Regusci Ranch, where the property and hospitality are legendary.

Opposite: The estate garden provided a spectacular setting for supper. Below: Built in 1878, Regusci's historic dairy and cattle ranch is now a world-class winery. Visitors experience breathtaking views, remarkable wines, and traces of the past at this pre-Prohibition "ghost winery."

Clockwise, from top: At the Regusci farm stand, visitors can purchase fresh organic produce on the honor system throughout the year and are encouraged to tour the two-acre estate garden. Opposite: Jim and Laura Regusci with their horses Fancy and Rooster and dog Ruby.

Jim and Laura Regusci

At age nineteen, Jim started his own vineyard management business with one truck and a strong will. Today, his business farms more than 1,500 acres. He and his wife, Laura—who taught organic farming, gardening, and viticulture at the local junior college and high school—maintain the family heritage of farming. Together, they grow not only wine grapes, but also produce olive oil, raise livestock, and cultivate fruits, flowers, nuts, and vegetables.

"Jim and I have a passion for sharing the beauty and bounty of this property. We enjoy our wines the most when they are paired with the food we grow and people we love."

—LAURA REGUSCI

Regusci Ranch Wedge Salad

Makes 8 servings

- 1 cup mayonnaise
- 1 cup sour cream
- 1 cup chopped fresh parsley
- ¼ cup chopped fresh chives
- ¼ cup chopped fresh basil
- 2 teaspoons chopped fresh dill
- 1½ teaspoons fresh lemon zest
- 1 teaspoon garlic powder
- 1 teaspoon onion powder

- 1 teaspoon salt
- 2 large heads iceberg lettuce
- 1 cucumber, sliced
- 2 large heirloom tomatoes, sliced or chopped
- 1 cup cooked and crumbled applewood smoked bacon
- ½ cup crumbled gorgonzola cheese

Combine mayonnaise, sour cream, parsley, chives, basil, dill, lemon zest, garlic powder, onion powder, and salt in a bowl, stirring until well blended. Cover and chill until ready to serve.

Cut each head of lettuce into 4 wedges and place on serving plates. Spoon dressing over lettuce wedges. Top evenly with cucumber, tomatoes, bacon, and cheese.

Menu

Regusci Ranch Wedge Salad
Crumbled gorgonzola, garden vegetables, applewood smoked bacon
The Elders Estate Cabernet Sauvignon

Smoked Pork Tenderloin
Cherry and Fig Compote, garlic mashed potatoes, romano beans, crispy shallots
Patriarch Estate Proprietary Red Blend

Homemade Tiramisu
Chocolate Bourbon-Dipped S'mores
Handmade Chocolates
Angelo's Estate Cabernet Sauvignon

Opposite: Chef Angel Perez's family has been farming with Jim for thirty years. Nearly every ingredient in Angel's salad was harvested on the property. Clockwise from top left: Flatware was placed in a pruning sheer holster. Laura holds Gypsy, a Buff Orpington rooster. Wine barrels served as tables for a vertical display of appetizers, and three estate cabernet sauvignon. The lovely but simple table setting was a reflection of the garden.

Smoked Pork Tenderloin with Cherry and Fig Compote

Makes 8 servings

2 cups firmly packed light brown sugar
½ cup kosher salt
8 cups water
2 cinnamon sticks
1 tablespoon red pepper flakes
1 yellow or white onion, coarsely chopped
4 celery stalks, cut into 1-inch pieces
1 carrot, peeled and cut into 1-inch pieces
6 garlic cloves, crushed
2 bay leaves
2 (1¼- to 1½-pound) pork tenderloins, trimmed
Cherry and Fig Compote

Combine sugar, salt, water, cinnamon sticks, pepper flakes, onion, celery, carrot, garlic, and bay leaves in a large pot. Bring mixture to a boil. Reduce heat to medium-low and simmer for 20 to 25 minutes. Remove from heat and cool to room temperature. Set aside 1 cup brine liquid for Cherry and Fig Compote.

Add pork to brine. Cover and refrigerate for 6 to 8 hours. Drain pork, discarding brine. Prepare smoker according to manufacturer's directions. Smoke pork at 225 degrees for 1½ to 2 hours or until thermometer inserted in thickest portion reads 145 degrees. Transfer to a cutting board and let rest for 5 minutes. Slice pork and serve with Cherry and Fig Compote.

Note: You can also grill pork tenderloins over medium-high heat for 12 to 15 minutes or until pork reaches 140 degrees, turning occasionally. Let rest for 5 minutes (meat will continue to cook as it rests).

CHERRY AND FIG COMPOTE

1 cup reserved brine
½ cup butter, cut into pieces
1 medium white onion, diced
3 garlic cloves, thinly sliced
3 cups pitted fresh cherries
1 cinnamon stick
4 teaspoons ground cumin
¼ teaspoon chopped fresh thyme
¼ teaspoon freshly ground black pepper
1/16 teaspoon ground cloves
12 fresh figs, trimmed and quartered

Pour brine into a small saucepan over medium heat. Bring to a boil. Reduce heat and simmer for 8 minutes or until reduced to ½ cup. Set aside.

Melt butter in a large skillet over medium heat. Add onion and garlic and cook for 4 to 5 minutes or until onions are translucent. Stir in cherries, cinnamon stick, cumin, thyme, pepper, and cloves. Cook for 2 to 4 minutes or until cherries are tender, stirring frequently. Stir in brine reduction and cook for 1 minute. Add figs and cook for 2 minutes. Makes 3¾ cups.

Opposite: The pork that was served as the main course was raised on the ranch. Right from top: Set beside the firepit were all the makings for s'mores, as well as tiramisu in Mason jars and chocolate bourbon sauce.

Paying Homage to Mother Nature

A winding road that climbs far above the valley floor into the Vaca Mountains leads visitors to the hallowed ground of Pritchard Hill and Chappellet Vineyard. Among a small group of pioneering families to begin making wine after Prohibition, the Chappellets have been farming their rugged terroir since 1967.

One fall day, winery founder Molly Chappellet invited friends for a walk in her celebrated garden, followed by brunch. Walking down the citrus path, her guests plucked oranges from the trees; listened to a hawk cry under the majestic oak; and when they reached the meadow, paused to admire the expansive views of the valley. The walk concluded in a Zen-like garden. Giant boulders spaced over a quiet mesa of black pumice set the stage for brunch overlooking the vineyards.

A massive moss-covered stone served as the buffet. Instead of tables or chairs, Molly used stumps, rocks, and benches made from fallen trees as seats or spots to rest cups of coffee or glasses of wine. On this day, she recruited her eldest son, Cyril, now CEO of the winery, to cook his father's legendary waffles. These waffles were served with baked apples from the orchard, homemade apricot jam, and thick slabs of bacon. As guests settled in amongst the boulders, Molly shared the history of Pritchard Hill and how she and Donn made a life for their family and built the winery. Her pride in her family's world-class cabernet sauvignon was evident—as was her love for her six children, who are all engaged in the business.

"The gifts we get from nature never cease to take my breath away," says Molly, who spends much of her time nurturing her garden or reflecting on the beauty of Pritchard Hill. It captured her soul fifty years ago, and her passion for the property hasn't waned. Time spent immersed in the beauty of the Chappellet estate is unforgettable. Experiencing it with Molly gave her guests a deeper appreciation not only for the estate's wines, but also for the powerful influence nature has on winemaking and living.

Below: Visitors are welcome by appointment to Chappellet's "cathedral of wine," a timeless pyramid shaped building constructed in 1968. Opposite: Guests enjoy waffles for brunch and an expansive view of Lake Hennessy and the valley below.

Donn's Waffles

Makes 1 dozen

Donn Chappellet perfected this recipe nearly forty years ago. His sons, Cyril, Jon Mark, and Dominic, have all mastered their Dad's waffle-making technique to keep his breakfast legacy alive. The trick to these irresistibly light and crisp waffles is tossing them from hand to hand when they come out of the waffle iron. Serving each waffle immediately is essential.

- 2 jumbo egg yolks
- 1 cup all-purpose flour
- 1 teaspoon baking soda
- 1 cup sour cream
- 2 rounded tablespoons polenta or coarsely ground cornmeal

- 3 cups buttermilk
- 5 tablespoons butter, melted
- 3 jumbo egg whites
  Nonstick cooking spray

Preheat a Belgian-style waffle iron.

Combine egg yolks, flour, baking soda, sour cream and polenta in a large mixing bowl. Add buttermilk gradually, stirring until blended. Stir in melted butter (do not over mix). Beat egg whites in a clean bowl with an electric mixer until stiff peaks form. Fold egg whites gently into batter with a rubber spatula (do not over mix).

Coat waffle iron with cooking spray. Pour about ⅔ cup batter to cover waffle grid (do not overflow). Close iron and cook for 5 to 6 minutes or until steam stops coming from the iron.

Quickly flip the waffle back and forth between your hands to crisp and cool slightly.

Serve with topping of choice.

Above: Chappellet's Signature Chenin Blanc honors Molly. Right: Donn's Waffles were served on ceramic plates hand crafted by a local potter.

Molly Chappellet

Moving to Pritchard Hill from Beverly Hills in 1967, Molly founded Chappellet Vineyards with her late husband, Donn, becoming the first to build a winery above the valley floor since the 1930s. She is a mother of six, grandmother of eleven, and a great-grandmother—as well as a master gardener, an artist, and the author of five books.

"Sharing the ever-changing excitement of nature is one of the greatest joys of living on Pritchard Hill. There's a poetic feeling that transcends place." —MOLLY CHAPPELLET

Above: Fruit picked from the orchard and vineyard on Pritchard Hill was part of the brunch set on a massive boulder.

Molly's Baked Apples

Makes 6 servings

A variety of apples grow in Molly's orchard; some she inherited and others she purposely planted. Baked apples are a staple at breakfast or brunch in her home. The baking method depends on the variety of apple. She picks Red Delicious apples before they are fully ripe and quarters, cores, and bakes them with a little brown sugar, lemon, and butter. Her favorite heirloom apples are baked whole with a little butter. She prefers to bake Roma Beauty apples cored and stuffed.

6 large Roma Beauty apples	1 teaspoon ground cinnamon
½ cup chopped pecans	6 tablespoons butter
½ cup packed brown sugar	¾ cup water
2 tablespoons raisins	

Preheat oven to 375 degrees.

Wash and core apples, leaving ½ inch of core at the bottom to contain the filling; opening should be large enough for ample filling.

Combine pecans, brown sugar, raisins, and cinnamon in a small bowl and mix well. Press a portion of mixture into each apple to fill core. Dot apples with butter. Fill a pie plate with about ¾ cup water or enough to cover the bottom. Arrange apples upright in pie plate. Bake for 1 hour or until apples are soft and filling is browned.

Note: If Roma Beauty apples are not available, Gala or Fuji apples are recommended.

Nature's Centerpiece

No matter the time of year, taking a walk outside and keeping a watchful eye can identify something unusual to use on your table. "Foraging is more spontaneous, creative, and fun than visiting a florist," says Molly. "The pleasure is in the looking, the selecting, and the collecting." She delights in letting the land inspire her, creating a link between the indoors and the outdoors on her dining table and in her home.

Wherever you live—in the city, at the beach, in the desert—look around. Even beneath your feet, you can find treasures (nature's gifts), such as seed pods, stones, driftwood, a broken branch. When you bring these earthy treasures away from their natural habitat, you'll discover all sorts of possibilities for interesting new uses. Elegance is derived from simplicity.

Left: Perfectly cooked baked apples.

Following pages: A Zen-like garden of boulders was the setting for brunch.

Handcrafted Melodies

Opposite: A stunning fall vineyard was the backdrop for a bountiful luncheon buffet. Below: A collection of American Luthier handcrafted guitars decorates Gargiulo's stylish tasting salon. Visitors are welcome to taste—and perhaps play—by appointment.

Guitar riffs are often heard streaming out from the tasting room at Gargiulo Vineyards' Money Road Ranch. Built from an old bridge, basketball court floors, and other repurposed materials, Gargiulo's tasting room is a showplace for sustainability, wine, and guitars. The collection of handcrafted American Luthier guitars on display underscores the importance of artisans in making guitars and wine. Recognized as one of Napa Valley's first-growth wine estates, Gargiulo Vineyards has crafted collectible cabernet sauvignon since 1999.

One fall, proprietors Jeff and Valerie Gargiulo provided guests with a memorable and melodic experience, holding an Italian-inspired luncheon on the terrace. Gazing at sweeping views of Napa Valley, guests sat at a long table decorated with fresh produce, bread, cheese, and olive oil. In the midst of the table was a bowl of rich red rock and clay soil from the vineyard, underscoring the importance of terroir in winemaking. A pair of whimsical ceramic birds, gifted to Valerie by the late Margrit Mondavi, was nestled in and around the dirt. The table also featured pottery bowls holding pears and figs— treasures from cousins and pioneering Napa grape farmers Barney and Belle Rhodes. "Remembering those who paved the way is important," says Valerie. "It honors their legacy and brings them back into our lives."

The menu was based on what was in season. Jeff prepared a sumptuous meal of grilled lamb, chicken, and figs, plus a superb eggplant and tomato dish served buffet style. His Evo Lamb Chops are the specialty of the house. "They will make you weep," says Jeff, "especially when paired with G Major 7 Cabernet Sauvignon."

Music is always part of the experience at Gargiulo. Jeff, who has played guitar since he was thirteen, performs as a member of the Silverado Pickups. "When you drink wine," he says, "you're relaxed and want to listen to music. It's an authentic experience." As dessert was served, Jeff picked up a 1945 Martin guitar and played several songs. His stream-of-consciousness lyrics captured the spirit of the afternoon and paid homage to his guests. The songs were unique, artistic, and from the heart, just like the Gargiulos and their wines.

Jeff and Valerie Gargiulo

Aself-described "fruit peddler," Jeff Gargiulo has been farming most of his life. His previous company, Gargiulo, Inc., produced, packed, marketed, and distributed fruits and vegetables. Jeff served as the CEO of Sunkist Growers and is now chairman of Greenleaf Produce, a San Francisco–based produce distributor. Bitten by the wine bug, he and Valerie purchased their first vineyard in 1992. The Gargiulos split their time between Oakville, California, and Naples, Florida, and are actively involved in charitable organizations in both states. As chairs of Auction Napa Valley and Naples Winter Wine Festival, they have raised over $147 million for charity.

"Harmony is the essence of life, with all the elements in balance. This is true in music and in wine. I find harmony in the diversity of Napa Valley, a place that epitomizes the art of living."

—JEFF GARGIULO

Lemon Chicken

Makes 4 servings

There are many versions of Lemon Chicken, and this is a classic dish on the Amalfi coast in Italy, where fresh lemons are abundant.

- ¼ cup kosher salt
- 4 cups water
- 4 boneless, skin-on chicken breasts
- ¼ cup fresh lemon juice
- 1 tablespoon Dijon mustard
- ¼ cup olive oil plus more for drizzling

- 1–2 teaspoons chopped fresh rosemary plus more for garnish
- Kosher salt and freshly ground black pepper to taste
- 2 lemons, sliced

Combine salt and water in a large bowl, stirring until salt dissolves. Add chicken; cover and chill for 1 to 2 hours. Drain; rinse chicken and pat dry.

Whisk lemon juice, mustard, ¼ cup olive oil, and 1 to 2 teaspoons rosemary in a small bowl. Stir in salt and pepper. Arrange chicken in a baking dish. Pour marinade over chicken, turning to coat. Cover and chill for 2 hours. Drain chicken and let stand at room temperature for 30 minutes.

Preheat oven to 375 degrees. Heat a large cast-iron or heavy skillet over medium-high heat. Sear lemons on both sides until browned. Set aside. Sear chicken for 3 minutes per side. Transfer skillet to oven and bake for 15 minutes or until chicken is cooked through. Spoon pan drippings over chicken and drizzle with olive oil. Serve with lemon slices and garnish with rosemary.

Above: Edible elements, including bread, cheese, olive oil, and produce, are always part of the centerpiece on Jeff and Valerie's table. Left: Grilled lemons and fresh rosemary artfully garnish a platter of chicken.

Evo Lamb Chops with Lemon and Rosemary

Makes 4 servings

Evo is a fabulous flat-topped or plancha grill that gets incredibly hot fast, with an even temperature. A hot good cast-iron skillet will work, as well as your favorite grill. Frenching the rack means removing the fat and meat on the ends of the rib bones. Use a thin knife or ask your butcher to do it for you.

1 (8-bone) rack of lamb, frenched and cut into chops
Kosher salt and freshly ground black pepper to taste

¼ cup olive oil
2 tablespoons minced fresh rosemary
1 tablespoon fresh lemon juice

Sprinkle lamb chops with salt and pepper and arrange in a dish. Whisk olive oil, rosemary, and lemon juice in a small bowl and brush over chops. Cover and chill for 2 hours.

Let lamb chops stand at room temperature for 30 minutes before cooking.

Heat Evo or a large cast-iron skillet to medium-high heat. Cook chops for 3 to 4 minutes per side for medium-rare or to desired degree of doneness. Transfer to a platter; let rest for 5 minutes.

Rock Collides with Wine

As music aficionados, who have entertained many Grammy award-winning artists in their home, Jeff and Valerie Gargiulo look forward to Memorial Day weekend each year. For three days, music legends descend on Napa Valley to perform at BottleRock Napa Valley. With five stages, more than ninety performers, wine, food, and craft brews, the festival attracts nearly 100,000 fans annually. Headliners have included Florence + the Machine, No Doubt, Imagine Dragons, Stevie Wonder, Eric Church, Robert Plant, and Blues Traveler. Jeff and his band, the Silverado Pickups, take the stage annually. When he isn't performing, he and Valerie can be found on the VIP Skydeck, rocking to tunes and sharing their remarkable wines.

Opposite: Gargiulo's rockabilly band, the Silverado Pickups, take the stage at BottleRock. Italian ceramics were used to present the Evo Lamb Chops. Above: To pay homage to their terroir, the Gargiulos placed a bowl of dirt from Money Road Ranch as the focal point of the table. Valerie plucked leaves from a nearby tree to use as place cards.

Baked Eggplant with Tomatoes

Makes 6 servings

The inspiration for this dish is the island of Lipari, the largest of the Aeolian Islands off the northern coast of Sicily. Use an Italian brand of tomatoes. There are big differences in sweetness, but I prefer the ones with no added citric acid.

- 2 tablespoons olive oil plus more for drizzling
- 4 garlic cloves, peeled
- 2 (28-ounce) cans peeled whole tomatoes
  Kosher salt and freshly ground black pepper to taste
- 3 eggplant
- 6 large eggs

- 3½ cups fresh breadcrumbs
- 1 cup (4 ounces) freshly grated Pecorino Romano cheese, divided
- 2 cups (8 ounces) fresh mozzarella cheese, crumbled
- 4 large ripe tomatoes, sliced
  Fresh basil leaves

Heat 2 tablespoons olive oil in a large saucepan over medium heat. Add garlic and cook for 2 minutes. Stir in tomatoes and cook for 3 minutes or until warm. Pour mixture in batches into a food mill or blender and purée until smooth, pouring into a bowl. Return to saucepan and add salt and pepper. Cook over medium-low heat for 1 to 1½ hours or until reduced by ⅓ and sauce is slightly thickened. Set aside.

Meanwhile, peel eggplant and slice ⅛ to ¼ inch thick. Arrange in a single layer on rimmed baking sheets and sprinkle both sides with salt. Let stand for 1 hour.

Preheat oven to 400 degrees. Break eggs into a shallow bowl; beat until well blended. Place breadcrumbs in another shallow bowl.

Pat eggplant dry with paper towels. Dip in eggs, shaking gently to remove excess, and coat with breadcrumbs. Arrange in a single layer on lightly greased rimmed baking sheets. Drizzle with olive oil. Bake for 10 minutes and turn over. Bake for 10 to 12 minutes or until golden brown. Sprinkle with salt.

Spread ⅓ of sauce over bottom of lightly greased 9x13-inch baking dish. Layer half the eggplant over sauce. Spread a third of the sauce over eggplant and sprinkle evenly with half the Romano. Sprinkle evenly with mozzarella. Add remaining half of the eggplant and remaining sauce. Layer top with tomatoes. Sprinkle with remaining Romano, salt, and pepper. Drizzle lightly with olive oil.

Bake, loosely covered with foil, for 15 minutes. Bake, uncovered, for 25 minutes or until hot and bubbly. Let rest for 20 minutes before serving. Top each serving with basil.

Note: The breadcrumbs can get damp and clump together after coating several eggplant slices. If that happens, stir in 1 tablespoon dried breadcrumbs to make breadcrumb mixture drier.

Opposite: Inspiration for Jeff's eggplant dish came from a lunch in Italy. Right from top: Jeff plays a 1945 Martin and composes a song for guests: "One more glass of wine and you'll be singing with me." Gargiulo's signature wine, named G Major 7 after a classic jazz guitar chord, stands next to the historic Martin guitar.

Three Perfect Dates

A cowgirl sculpture welcomes visitors to Phifer Pavitt's century-old barn turned winery. Symbolic of a bygone era and aptly named Moxie, she captures the spirit of the brand: approachable, strong, feminine, and authentic.

To unwind after harvest, proprietor Suzanne Phifer Pavitt indulged in three of her favorite dates: she invited girlfriends over to enjoy brunch and yoga, took her family on an overnight camping adventure, and spent a romantic evening at home by the fire with Shane, her husband of eighteen years. Making dates with people she treasures is important to Suzanne. "Cherish the moments you have together," she often says, "because life doesn't come with a pause button."

Time with her yogini girlfriends was restorative. Nearly 100 hurricane candles provided an atmosphere of peace, and the dining table was draped with a garland of calming eucalyptus. The group nibbled on quiche and English muffins from The Model Bakery and sipped sauvignon blanc. After brunch, the table was moved and yoga commenced. To Suzanne, it was the ideal way to catch up with her girlfriends.

Suzanne also unplugged with Shane and her two teenage sons, Jackson and Rhett. She planned an overnight camping date, loading their Airstream with goodies to make supper around the campfire. Without the distractions of electronics, work, and homework, they grilled burgers, sipped hot cocoa, made s'mores, and, most importantly, enjoyed conversation together.

For a quintessentially romantic date with Shane, Suzanne chose to stay home. Coq au vin simmered in a slow cooker, while the table in front of the fire was set with roses and candles. She and Shane wrote a note of gratitude to share at dinner and dressed for a black-tie affair. They opened a bottle of cabernet from their library and ended the evening dancing to their favorite song.

Each date ignited a different fire in Suzanne's soul: calming candles and yoga with the girls, family time around a comforting campfire, and roaring flames to heat up the romance at home. For Suzanne, nothing could be more perfect.

Below: A Napa Green Certified winery, Phifer Pavitt calls this reclaimed and updated barn home. Visitors are welcome by appointment to taste their artisan-crafted wines in a stylish salon setting. They can also share their own date-night stories on a blackboard wall in the tasting room. Opposite: A stunning setting for a brunch date with girlfriends.

Date Night Bounty Apple Butter

Makes 7 cups

Use your favorite organic apples and add a splash of bourbon for bolder flavor. Serve on scones, muffins, biscuits, or pork chops, or stir into yogurt.

- 6 pounds organic Jonathan, Honeycrisp, Winesap, or other firm apples
- ½ cup sugar
- ½ cup firmly packed light brown sugar
- 1 teaspoon ground nutmeg
- ¼ teaspoon ground cloves
- ¼ teaspoon ground cardamom
- ¼ teaspoon salt
- 1 tablespoon vanilla extract

Core and slice apples (no need to peel). Place in a 6-quart slow cooker. Combine sugar, brown sugar, nutmeg, cloves, cardamom, and salt in a small bowl; stir into apples. Cook on Low for 10 hours or until apples are very soft and dark brown, stirring occasionally.

Process apple mixture in a food mill or purée with an immersion blender until very smooth. Stir in vanilla. Return apple mixture to slow cooker, if necessary. Cook, uncovered, on Low for 2 to 3 hours or until thickened. Spoon into sterile canning jars or freezer containers, leaving at least 1-inch headspace. Cover and refrigerate for up to 2 weeks or freeze for up to 1 year.

Opposite: Phifer Pavitt and her girlfriends strike a pose. Left: Brunch guests received a jar of homemade Apple Butter to take home. Above: Personalized menus doubled as place cards. The "agenda" was beautifully hand painted.

Clockwise from above: Suzanne dressed up their campsite table with a bouquet of greens, berries, and roses. All the fixings for s'mores and hot cocoa made for the perfect camping date. The spread included local cheeses, breadsticks, and charcuterie from Panevino. Opposite: The boys get the campfire burning.

Suzanne Phifer Pavitt and Shane Pavitt

A Georgia native, Suzanne moved to California to obtain her MBA. Shane grew up in California, attending college in Arizona before returning to his home state. Both were deep into their respective careers in technology sales and finance when they fell in love in 1997. A year later, Suzanne and Shane were married; two years later, they purchased land in Napa Valley; and five years later, they decided to commit to a bucolic life, moving to Napa to become full-time vintners.

"Be adventurous and create intentional 'dates' that inspire and entertain the people you treasure. Cherish those moments together because life doesn't come with a pause button!"

—SUZANNE PHIFER PAVITT

Recipe for a Romantic and Exciting Date Night

Makes 2 happy people

Suzanne and Shane make time for each other by having at least one date night a month. It gives them time to reflect on their lives and helps to keep the flame burning bright in their relationship. "Making the effort to create a romantic evening for the love of your life in the home you have built together is far more meaningful than a night out on the town," says Suzanne. Here is her "recipe" for a dreamy date at home.

A ROMANTIC AND EXCITING DATE NIGHT

- Set a date and time
- Plan a spectacular dinner menu. Reduce time in the kitchen by selecting a satiating dish that can simmer in a slow cooker for hours. Try braised short ribs or coq au vin; both are delicious with a big Napa Valley cabernet like Date Night.
- Pick up recipe ingredients at the market. Keep them simple to take full advantage of the time together
- Take care of meal preparations the night before
- Write gratitude cards to each other
- Pick up fresh flowers
- Set a romantic table using fancy china, beautiful linens, fresh flowers, and candles
- Remove dining chairs and add a love seat or settee so you can sit together—just like you might on a first date

DATE NIGHT DIRECTIONS

On the night of your date, put any finishing touches on the dreamy setting you've created. While dinner cooks, dress for a fiery evening. Select an outfit that says wow. Greet your dinner date with a meaningful kiss. Pop the cork on some bubbles. Toast each other. Nibble on caviar, smoked salmon, foie gras, or your favorite hors d'oeuvre. Hold hands. During the meal, keep the conversation focused on love; don't stray to children, work, or friends. Sneak in a kiss or two. Present your gratitude cards and read them aloud. Expand on the areas that reinforce appreciation and attraction. Put on some music, clear the table, kick off your heels, and dance. Forget the dishes—leave them in the sink.

Clockwise from top: Suzanne and Shane shared notes of gratitude. What could be better than Date Night wines on a date night? The couple sat shoulder to shoulder at a romantic table for two.

Desmond Echavarrie: One of just 230 Master Sommeliers in the world, Des is a veteran of award-winning restaurants, such as The French Laundry. He runs Scale Wine Group, a Napa-based wine marketing company.

Demystifying Decanting

The question, "Would you like me to decant the wine?" is not always easy to answer. To eliminate some of the guesswork, Master Sommelier Desmond "Des" Echavarrie explains the reasons for decanting red wine.

Aged Red Wine

When serving an older wine (more than fifteen years old), decanting serves to separate clear wine from sediment. While sediment is perfectly acceptable, many people prefer not to drink (or chew) it. Decanting an old wine immediately before serving is what Des recommends.

Young Red Wine

Decanting a young wine (less than five years old) serves to aerate it. A full-bodied Napa Valley cabernet sauvignon benefits from having contact with air prior to drinking. The wine will become perceptibly more approachable and fruitful with the incorporation of air through decanting. Des advises decanting a young wine four hours before service, tasting the wine every hour to look for changes. If the wine is improving, leave it in the decanter longer. When the wine starts to plateau, funnel it back into the bottle and replace the cork to restrict exposure to oxygen. If time is limited, an aeration device that uses the Venturi principle, quickly mixing air and wine together, can be a substitute for decanting a young wine.

Selecting a Decanter

Decanters, like wine lovers, come in all shapes and sizes. Some decanters are much easier to pour from, while others have a greater surface area for wine to contact air. They all do the same job. Des says, "Pick one that matches your personal style." His favorite decanter is an old-school Riedel duck. When it's filled with one of his favorite wines, it is one lucky duck!

"Even though it can sometimes seem like a big dog and pony show, decanting is often necessary. It really does improve the experience and enjoyment of a special bottle of wine."

—DESMOND ECHAVARRIE, MASTER SOMMELIER

Life Is A Cabernet

A white wooden water tower has become a Napa Valley icon. Appearing on the label of Silver Oak for more than four decades, the tower is synonymous with outstanding cabernet sauvignon. In 1972, Ray Duncan and business partner Justin Meyer made a bold move, building a winery around just one varietal, cabernet sauvignon. Their risk paid off, and they quickly made their mark as one of Napa's first "cult" wines.

It is not uncommon for Ray's son and Silver Oak proprietor David Duncan to entertain two nights in a row, particularly during harvest season. One week, during the throes of crush, David hosted an intimate group in front of the wine library for a formal dinner. The following evening, friends joined him for an al fresco supper, prepared in the winery's wood oven. He prefers "casual elegance" when entertaining and is grateful to have winery chef Dominic Orsini in the kitchen.

Surrounded by hundreds of bottles of wine in the glasshouse library, guests enjoyed a multi-course meal with four vintages of cabernet sauvignon. The table was set simply to allow the setting and the wines to take the stage. David enjoys serving several vintages at the same time. "It's a lesson in history as well as in wine aging," says David. "Every year has its own story and personality."

The following evening, friends gathered on the winery terrace under a canopy made from vines of hops. A rustic yet elegant table was set for a family-style supper, which was cooked in a wood oven. Guests watched Chef Orsini toss dough and assemble delicious pizzas. He also roasted whole chickens and vegetables in the oven. Later that evening, everyone gathered around the firepit while David played his guitar, taking requests as the group sang along and sipped cabernet.

David enjoys being with guests and hearing their "bottle stories" of special moments celebrated over a bottle of Silver Oak. For him, the phrase "Life Is A Cabernet" is more than his winery motto—it is a way of life.

Below: Silver Oak's water tower is a Napa Valley landmark. Visitors are welcomed daily and appointments are recommended for tours, vertical tastings, and food and wine pairings. Opposite: Dinner in the glasshouse wine library at a table accented with autumn colors.

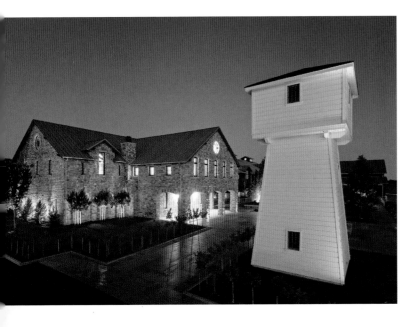

Above: Chef Orsini's signature Filet Mignon garnished with nasturtium from the winery garden.

Opposite, from top: Custom dishes used to serve dinner were decorated with the winery's iconic

water tower. The water tower was also featured in house-made chocolates that were served after

dinner. An impressive fall display of pumpkins and gourds, all grown in the winery garden.

Filets Mignons à la Orsini

Makes 6 servings

This dish is classically known as Tournedos Rossini, named after the nineteenth century composer Gioachino Rossini. With the name so similar to my last name, I couldn't resist the temptation to make it my own: grilled filet mignon topped with a decadent slice of seared foie gras and shavings of elusive black truffle. Remember to prepare the Potato Gratin several hours to one day ahead.

6 (1-ounce) slices foie gras
  Fine sea salt and freshly ground black pepper to taste
1 tablespoon canola oil
6 (5- to 6-ounce) filets mignons
1 teaspoon extra-virgin olive oil
¾ cup (2 ounces) chanterelle mushrooms, cut into bite-size pieces

1–2 tablespoons chopped fresh sage
½ cup beef demi-glace
¼ cup Cognac
  Potato Gratin
  Shaved fresh black truffle
2 tablespoons finely chopped fresh chives
  Fleur de sel to taste

Preheat oven to 350 degrees.

Heat a large cast-iron skillet over high heat. Sprinkle foie gras with salt and pepper. Sear each slice for 30 to 45 seconds on one side only. Transfer to a plate, seared side up, and let rest at room temperature.

Wipe skillet; heat canola oil in skillet over high heat. Sprinkle steaks with salt and pepper; sear for 3 to 4 minutes per side. Transfer steaks to a baking sheet and top each steak with a slice of foie gras. Set aside.

Wipe skillet; heat olive oil in skillet over medium-high heat. Add mushrooms and sage; cook for 3 minutes or until mushrooms are tender, stirring constantly. Add demi-glace and Cognac, stirring until well blended. Simmer sauce for 3 to 5 minutes or until it coats the back of a spoon. Set mushroom sauce aside and keep warm.

Bake Potato Gratin disks, uncovered, for 12 minutes. Bake steaks for 3 to 5 minutes for medium-rare or to desired degree of doneness.

Place a Potato Gratin disk in the center of each serving plate. Spoon about 2 tablespoons mushroom sauce around each gratin. Place a steak on top of each gratin. Shave black truffle evenly over steak. Sprinkle evenly with chives and fleur de sel.

POTATO GRATIN

2 pounds Yukon gold potatoes
1 cup heavy whipping cream
1 teaspoon fine sea salt

¼ teaspoon ground nutmeg
1 cup (4 ounces) shredded Gruyère cheese

Preheat oven to 350 degrees. Butter a 9x13-inch baking pan and line with parchment paper.

Cut potatoes on a mandolin into paper thin slices, about 1/16 inch thick. Rinse with cold water and drain in a colander. Combine potatoes, cream, salt, and nutmeg in a large bowl. Drain potatoes, reserving cream mixture.

Arrange potato slices in overlapping layers in prepared baking pan, drizzling each layer with cream mixture and sprinkling with cheese; discard any remaining cream mixture. Cover with parchment paper and aluminum foil. Bake for 45 to 60 minutes or until potatoes are tender. Cool on a wire rack for 30 minutes.

Place a 9x13-inch pan on top of the potatoes and top with 2 or 3 cans to weigh it down. Refrigerate for 4 hours or overnight. Cut 6 rounds from the pressed potatoes using a 3-inch cutter. Transfer disks to a baking sheet; cover and chill until ready to use. Makes 6 servings.

David Duncan

David began his career at his family's Duncan Oil. He worked his way up the ranks and eventually became the president. In 2002, his father, Ray, tapped him to move to Napa to run Silver Oak. He immediately said yes and hasn't looked back. Thanks to David's vision and hands-on style, Silver Oak has become an industry leader in innovation and sustainability. He is committed to continuous improvement and often says, "We have yet to make our best bottle."

Above from left: Jars of house-made persimmon jam were a place card and a gift from the host. Chairs made from wine barrel staves surrounded the firepit. Silver Oak's highly regarded cabernet. Opposite: The stunning tablescape was covered in rustic yet refined elements.

"To me, wine is fun and friends and family. It enriches our lives, and it's a part of bringing people together around the table." —DAVID DUNCAN

Fig and Prosciutto Pizza

Makes 2 (10-inch) pizzas

All-purpose flour
Cornmeal Pizza Dough
⅓ cup whole-milk ricotta cheese
2 tablespoons heavy cream
½ teaspoon fine sea salt
6 fresh figs, thinly sliced

8 thin slices prosciutto (about 3 ounces)
½ cup (2 ounces) freshly shredded
   mozzarella cheese
   Extra-virgin olive oil
2 cups baby arugula

Place a pizza stone on the second lowest oven rack and preheat oven to 500 degrees.

Spread flour generously on a pizza peel or line a rimless baking sheet with parchment paper. Place 1 dough ball on peel; sprinkle lightly with flour and press into a flat disk. Pick up edge of dough, allowing weight of dough to stretch it. Rotate hands around the edge of dough, turning it and allowing dough to stretch before rotating again. Repeat until dough is stretched to a 12-inch round or oval crust. Place dough in center of floured peel.

Whisk ricotta, cream, and salt in a small bowl. Spread half the ricotta mixture over dough, leaving a ½-inch border. Arrange half the figs and 4 slices prosciutto over ricotta mixture and sprinkle with ¼ cup mozzarella.

Slide pizza onto preheated pizza stone. Bake for 5 minutes; rotate pizza 180 degrees and turn on broiler. Broil for 4 to 5 minutes or until crust is crisp and golden brown.

Remove from oven and immediately brush crust with olive oil. Let stand for 2 to 3 minutes. Sprinkle 1 cup arugula over pizza and cut into wedges. Repeat with remaining dough and ingredients. Allow oven to return to 500 degrees before baking.

CORNMEAL PIZZA DOUGH

For extra flavor, transfer dough to a lightly oiled bowl, turning to coat, and refrigerate for 18 to 48 hours. Let stand at room temperature for 30 minutes before rolling.

1 cup warm water (100 to 110 degrees)
1 teaspoon extra-virgin olive oil
½ teaspoon active dry yeast
½ teaspoon honey

2½ cups unbleached all-purpose flour
2 tablespoons cornmeal
1 teaspoon fine sea salt

Combine water, olive oil, yeast, and honey in bowl of a stand mixer fitted with a dough hook. Let stand for 5 minutes. Add flour and cornmeal; mix at medium speed for 1 minute. Add salt; mix for 2 minutes.

Cover bowl with plastic wrap and let rise in a warm place (70 to 80 degrees) for 45 minutes. Punch dough down. Remove from bowl and fold in half; flatten dough and fold in half. Repeat and return dough to bowl. Cover and let rise in a warm place for 45 minutes.

Turn dough out onto a lightly floured work surface; dust dough lightly with flour. Divide in half and shape each piece into a ball. Cover with a damp towel and let rest at room temperature for 1 to 3 hours. Makes 2 (10-inch) pizza crusts.

Opposite: Fresh arugula from the garden was a key ingredient in the pizza. Right: Winery chef Dominic Orsini, author of *Life in a Cabernet Kitchen*, put on a show handcrafting pizzas for dinner guests.

MENU

CHARCUTERIE PLATE

House Smoked Salmon

CHEF'S CHEESE PLATE

PRIME RIB

BOUNTY HUNTER

RARE WINE & SPIRITS

Bounty of the Best

A landmark building in downtown Napa is home to one of the area's most recognized businesses: Bounty Hunter Rare Wine & Spirits. Bounty Hunter is the purveyor that many people—in Napa and around the country—seek when acquiring fine wines and spirits. To some, it's a producer of great wines and spirits. To others, it's a restaurant that serves hearty fare with a remarkable wine list. To all, it stands for the values of the West: honesty, integrity, trust, and the pursuit of the best.

A Saturday evening in September provided a perfect opportunity for Mark S. Pope, founder of Bounty Hunter, to gather friends and colleagues and open more than a few great bottles of wine. The evening began with the Boulevardier Cocktail, cheese, and charcuterie in the receiving room, under an American flag that once flew above the 9-11 memorial. Supper was served in the brick-walled dining room at a massive table with a centerpiece built from Western memorabilia. The vastness and scale of the West was depicted on the table. Everything was big—from a full wine barrelhead place mat at each setting to towering tree branches and bundles of grasses down the center. Taking in the elements, guests told colorful stories of the thrill of the hunt in pursuing the best wine and spirits. Dinner included heaping plates of Smoked Akaushi Prime Rib and hearty Bounty Hunter's Own Mac 'n' Cheese—the perfect accompaniments to a deep, dark glass of cabernet.

"Half the fun of throwing a party is provisioning the evening's hedonism," says Mark. He and the Bounty Hunter team members taste over 5,000 wines every year in search of the hottest wines in the world. They love sharing new discoveries with each other and their collectors. This evening, they popped the cork on a number of proprietary wines, including Blind Justice, Waypoint, and Pursuit, along with some recently discovered treasures and local favorites. As the wine flowed, a true esprit de corps emerged that reminded everyone why they love being together, especially in wine country.

The motto for Bounty Hunter is "People just want great stuff." The evening was all about great stuff, indeed—sharing the abundance and pleasure of Napa Valley living.

The Boulevardier Cocktail

Makes 1 serving

    3 ounces Sazerac rye whiskey
    1 ounce Alessio Vermouth
    ½ ounce Gran Classico Bitter
        Orange peel
        Bourbon-soaked cherry

Combine rye whiskey, Vermouth, and Bitter in an ice-filled glass, stirring until very cold. Strain into a chilled cocktail glass. Garnish with orange peel and cherry.

Above: Guests enjoyed the Boulevardier Cocktail. The Boulevardier is in essence a Negroni made with rye whiskey instead of gin.

Bourbon—American for Whiskey

Napa Valley residents and visitors don't always drink wine; in fact, they often order a cocktail. And those in the know usually drink American whiskey.

Like apple pie and baseball, bourbon is distinctly American. Over fifty years ago, the US Congress signed a resolution that legislated the use of "bourbon" on a whiskey label. This 1964 declaration stated that no other country could produce a whiskey and call it bourbon.

There are parallels between bourbon and wine. The most obvious is that both are aged in toasted oak barrels, imparting unique flavors. A true bourbon is aged in American oak for two or more years, while a Napa Valley cabernet sauvignon is typically aged in French oak for eighteen to twenty-four months. Some producers in the bourbon industry have recently been using wine barrels to age their bourbon. Aging bourbon in a cask used for red wine adds layers of dark fruit, wine, and spice. For instance, Bounty Hunter features Jefferson Reserve Pritchard Hill Cask and Groth Cask bourbons, which are finished in barrels from Napa Valley cabernet producers.

Those who want to enjoy America's native spirit should try the Boulevardier Cocktail (recipe at left) or another classic such as a Manhattan, Old Fashioned, Sazerac, or Mint Julep. Bounty Hunter recommends sipping a great bourbon neat—no ice, no fuss, just the way a cowboy on the range would drink it.

"*There is nothing better than breaking bread and drinking the great stuff with folks who have something to say. I like being with people who are real, who believe in old-school ethics, and give a damn.*" —MARK S. POPE

Mark S. Pope

A work opportunity brought former pharmaceutical sales executive Mark S. Pope to Napa Valley. He quickly fell in love with the place, food, wine, and people. In 1994, Mark launched a unique wine-selling enterprise—the Bounty Hunter Rare Wine & Provisions catalog, which gives people seeking the finest wines the chance to make new discoveries. Mark's luxury, blue-jeans lifestyle approach to marketing premium wine has since expanded to include proprietary wine and whiskey brands and a restaurant.

Menu

House-Smoked Salmon
Waypoint "Hudson Vineyard" Chardonnay

Local Cured Charcuterie Plate
Pursuit "Shake Ridge Vineyard" Syrah

Smoked Akaushi Prime Rib
Bounty Hunter's Own Mac 'n' Cheese
Southern-Style Baked Beans
Jalapeño Cornbread
Blind Justice "Beckstoffer To Kalon Vineyard"
Cabernet Sauvignon

Fall Fruit Bread Pudding
California Artisan Cheese Plate
Topaz "Late Harvest" Sauvignon Blanc/Semillon

Above: An individual serving of good ol' Mac 'n' Cheesee. Opposite, clockwise from top: A bounty

of wine and Western memorabilia—from mounts to books and boots—sparked conversation at the

table. The place mat for each guest was a wine barrelhead.

Bounty Hunter's Own Mac 'n' Cheese

Makes 10 to 12 servings

- 4 cups whole milk
- 3 bay leaves
- 1 pound elbow macaroni
- ½ cup unsalted butter
- 6 tablespoons all-purpose flour
- 2 teaspoons kosher salt
- ½ teaspoon freshly ground black pepper
- ⅛ teaspoon ground nutmeg
- 4 cups (16 ounces) shredded sharp cheddar cheese
- 1 cup (4 ounces) shredded Gruyère cheese
- 1 cup (4 ounces) shredded mozzarella cheese

Preheat oven to 350 degrees.

Heat milk and bay leaves in a saucepan over medium heat; keep warm. Cook pasta in boiling salted water in a large pot for 8 minutes or just until barely tender (do not overcook). Drain and set aside.

Melt butter in large pot over medium-low heat; whisk in flour until smooth. Cook for 1 minute, whisking constantly. Remove bay leaves from milk. Whisk milk gradually into flour mixture. Cook for 5 minutes or until thickened, whisking constantly. Remove from heat. Stir in salt, pepper, and nutmeg.

Combine cheeses in a large bowl. Add 2 cups cheese mixture to sauce, stirring until smooth. Stir pasta into sauce and pour into a buttered 9 x 13-inch baking dish. Top with remaining cheese mixture. Bake for 35 to 40 minutes or until golden brown and bubbly.

Smoked Akaushi Prime Rib

Serves 12

Chef Nick Heinrich swears by Akaushi Beef because he likes its marbling and tenderness. Meaning "red cow," Akaushi is a Japanese Wagyu breed of cattle. We commonly call it Kobe Beef but can really only use the term Kobe if the animal was raised in the Kobe region of Japan.

- 2 tablespoons kosher salt
- 1 tablespoon coarsely ground black pepper
- 1 (12- to 13-pound) bone-in rib-eye or standing rib roast

Combine salt and pepper in a bowl. Rub over roast and let stand at room temperature for 1 hour.

Soak hickory or oak wood chunks in water for at least 1 hour. Prepare charcoal fire in smoker; let burn for 15 to 20 minutes. Drain wood chunks and place on coals. Place water pan in smoker and add water to fill line. Add water periodically, if necessary, to reach fill line of smoker water pan.

Smoke roast at 250 degrees for 3½ to 4 hours or until a meat thermometer inserted into thickest portion registers 110 to 120 degrees. Transfer to a cutting board and cover loosely with foil. Let rest for 30 minutes before carving (roast will continue to cook as it rests).

To carve, remove bones in one piece by cutting along their contour. Slice meat across the grain.

Note: To roast in the oven, preheat oven to 325 degrees. Place prime rib, bone side down, in a deep roasting pan. Bake for 2 to 2½ hours or until a meat thermometer inserted into thickest portion registers 110 to 120 degrees.

Opposite: Chef Nick Heinrich, a southern boy from Alabama, smoked a full bone-in rib-eye for dinner. Above: Vintage cowboy hats and corkscrews were part of the evening's décor. A selection of Bounty Hunter's wine was served, including Blind Justice "Beckstoffer To Kalon Vineyard" Cabernet Sauvignon.

A Beautifully Wrapped Gift

One of Napa Valley's earliest wineries, Eshcol was established in 1886. Gene and Katie Trefethen purchased the property in 1968 and began replanting the vineyard. Their son John and his new wife, Janet, restored the historic building and produced the first wine under the Trefethen label in 1973.

Preparing a meal for friends has always brought joy to Janet, as she believes that wine is best when served with food. When she and John first came to Napa, it was a culinary desert. At that time, there were fewer than twenty-five wineries, and plums, prunes, and walnuts were the dominant crops. For Janet, entertaining at home was a must. Seeking to refine her culinary skills, she helped create the groundbreaking Napa Valley Cooking Class. For more than twenty years, the class brought together local women to learn from notable chefs and share ideas on entertaining and recipes.

One September evening, to celebrate the conclusion of their forty-ninth harvest, Janet and John gathered friends for supper at their home to toast the vintage. "To me," says Janet, "entertaining is like a gift. The table and atmosphere are the wrapping paper and ribbons, and the meal is the present inside."

To wrap the gift, Janet used fall colors to create a tablescape that was as abundant as the year's grape crop. Autumn leaves scattered densely on the table gave the sense of a forest floor. The leaves were topped with pumpkins, feathers, and bouquets of apricot-colored roses, hydrangeas, and sunflowers.

A beautifully roasted duck was the present, or main course, along with the salad, dessert, and sides prepared from fresh seasonal ingredients, including pomegranate, persimmon, pumpkin, and pear. As the daughter of a rice farmer, Janet always incorporates rice into her menus. This evening, she married grape farming and rice farming by having guests roll grape leaves and rice to make dolmas for the first course, while sipping Trefethen's Dry Riesling.

Janet's passion was evident during this evening of communal warmth and conviviality: from the atmosphere and décor to the delicious dinner, the time together was a gorgeous and unforgettable gift.

Below: The carefully restored Trefethen winery building was placed on the National Register of Historic Places as the only nineteenth-century wooden, gravity-flow winery surviving in Napa County. The Trefethens welcome visitors daily to taste their remarkable estate wines. Opposite: Janet presents an impeccably roasted duck.

Below and right: A salad with fall fruit. Roast duck with green and yellow cauliflower and butternut squash. Bottom: Making dolmas was a pre-dinner activity. Opposite, from top: The table setting showed the abundance of harvest and fall. All of the wines were poured from magnums.

Menu

Spooner Rice Dolmas
Estate Dry Riesling

Fall Salad of Kales
Estate Chardonnay

Cinderella Pumpkin Soup
Estate Harmony Chardonnay

Whole Roasted Duck with Black Trumpet
Mushrooms and Seasonal Vegetables
Estate Cabernet Sauvignon
Estate Dragon's Tooth Red Wine

Estate Pear Tart
Estate Late Harvest Riesling

Whole Roasted Duck with Black Trumpet Mushrooms and Seasonal Vegetables

Makes 4 to 6 servings

1 tablespoon Chinese five-spice
1 tablespoon ground cumin
1 teaspoon cayenne pepper
  Salt and freshly ground black pepper
  to taste
1 (5- to 6-pound) whole duck
  Boiling water
2 tablespoons butter, melted, divided

1 tablespoon olive oil
2 garlic cloves, minced
1 pound black trumpet or wild mushrooms,
  trimmed
1 (1½-pound) cauliflower, cut into florets
1 (2-pound) pumpkin or winter squash,
  peeled and cubed
2 tablespoons cabernet sauvignon

Preheat oven to 375 degrees. Combine five-spice, cumin, cayenne, salt, and black pepper in a small bowl; set aside.

Cut off wing tips and discard excess fat from duck. Fold neck skin under body and place duck, breast side up, on a wire rack in a deep roasting pan. Ladle about 2 cups boiling water over duck to tighten skin. Score breast lightly in a crosshatch pattern.

Drain water from inside duck cavity and drain the remaining water in pan. Pat duck dry with paper towels and tie legs together with kitchen twine. Rub duck evenly with spice mixture and place in a dry roasting pan.

Bake duck for 45 minutes. Spoon 1 tablespoon butter over duck and bake for 30 minutes. Spoon remaining 1 tablespoon butter over duck and bake for 30 minutes or until a meat thermometer inserted into thickest portion reaches 135 degrees. Cover with foil and let rest for 20 minutes. Maintain oven temperature.

Meanwhile, heat olive oil in a roasting pan over medium-high heat. Add garlic and cook for 30 seconds. Add mushrooms, cauliflower, and pumpkin, tossing to coat. Sprinkle with salt and black pepper. Cook for 5 to 8 minutes or just until starting to brown, stirring frequently. Stir in wine. Roast for 10 minutes or until vegetables are tender.

Arrange vegetables on a large platter, top with duck, and drizzle with pan drippings.

Janet Spooner Trefethen

With her sparkling personality, Janet has been marketing Trefethen wine since she and John produced their first vintage in 1973. She loves to educate people on wine and food pairings. As a result of her down-to-earth teaching style, Janet has been featured on *Good Morning America* with Julia Child and has delivered the commencement address at the Culinary Institute of America.

Supper on Spring Mountain

Wine connoisseurs seeking exceptional cabernet make Lokoya a destination. This remote and magnificent property, perched on the crest of Spring Mountain, features sweeping views of the valley and a stunning stone winery. Lokoya arguably produces some of Napa's most coveted and highly rated mountain cabernet sauvignon.

In November, winemaker Chris Carpenter gathered a group of collectors for an intimate dinner to preview soon-to-be-released wines and experience Lokoya's new winery. The castlelike building and surrounding estate was purchased in 2013. After three years of renovation, this spectacular structure—handcrafted from stone, concrete, and glass in the 1960s—is a museum to wine. The glass cellars showcase over two decades of Lokoya's cabernet sauvignon.

Prior to dinner, guests joined Chris for a tasting of current wines from Lokoya's four mountain appellations: Diamond Mountain District, Spring Mountain District, Howell Mountain, and Mount Veeder. The group discussed the ways in which the wines expressed the unique terroir, noting the intense individuality and powerful flavors present in each cabernet sauvignon. "The vines do the bulk of the work," says Chris. "My job is not to interfere and to let the fruit and terroir express themselves naturally and clearly."

Opposite: Rays of afternoon light add to the dramatic setting for dinner. Below: Built in the late 1960s and remodeled in 2016, the Lokoya estate is a reflection of artistry and craftsmanship in metal, stone, concrete, and glass. Visitors are welcomed by appointment, arranged with estate manager Bradley Wasserman.

This notion of not interfering—letting the wine and food shine—and of handcrafting carried over to dinner. There were no flowers on the table; instead, a collection of exquisite handblown Simon Pearce hurricanes formed the centerpiece. The two elegant beef dishes created by Chef Tracey Shepos Cenami were artfully displayed on hand-thrown ceramic plates, made by local potter Lynn Mahon. The two wines that Chris poured with dinner were truly magnum opus. Both received a perfect 100-point score from noted wine critic Robert Parker.

Experiencing four individual wines from four mountain appellations, in the grandeur of a stunning setting, surrounded by history, gave guests a look through Chris's lens. They left with a better understanding of Lokoya's philosophy: to strive for purity of flavor and balance, letting the fruit from each region express itself fully.

Right: This medieval-inspired concrete-framed window was designed by Fred Aves, who built the estate in the 1960s. Below: A modern glass gallery displays over twenty vintages of Lokoya's mountain cabernet sauvignon.

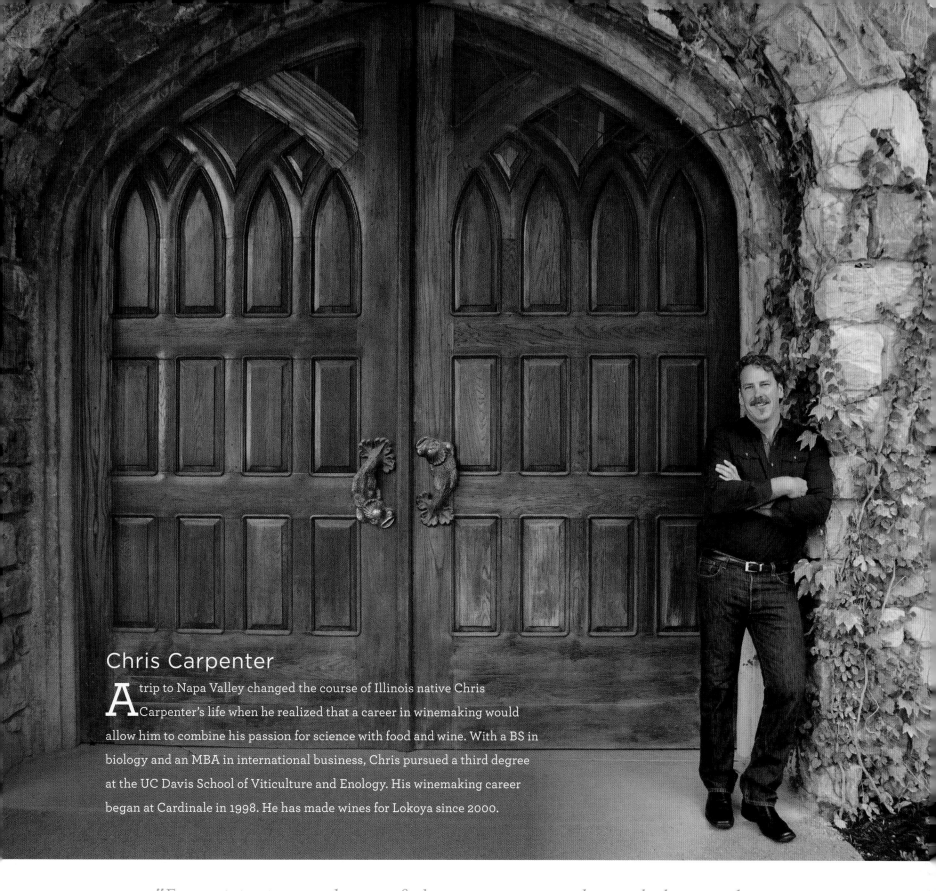

Chris Carpenter

A trip to Napa Valley changed the course of Illinois native Chris Carpenter's life when he realized that a career in winemaking would allow him to combine his passion for science with food and wine. With a BS in biology and an MBA in international business, Chris pursued a third degree at the UC Davis School of Viticulture and Enology. His winemaking career began at Cardinale in 1998. He has made wines for Lokoya since 2000.

"Entertaining is not only part of who we are as winemakers and why we make wine, it also allows me to observe the emotional response of what we have created in real time and over time." —CHRIS CARPENTER

Red Wine–Braised Short Ribs with Butternut Squash and Sautéed Greens

Makes 4 servings

5 pounds bone-in beef short ribs	2 carrots, diced
Kosher salt and freshly ground black pepper to taste	2 celery stalks, diced
1 sprig of fresh thyme	1 onion, diced
1 tablespoon whole black peppercorns	2 slices bacon, finely diced
1 tablespoon whole allspice	2 tablespoons tomato paste
1 bay leaf	3 cups cabernet sauvignon or other red wine
1 cinnamon stick	8 cups veal or beef stock or broth
1–2 tablespoons rice, canola, or other neutral-flavored oil	Butternut Squash
	Sautéed Greens

Sprinkle ribs with salt and pepper; let stand at room temperature for 30 minutes. Cut a 6-inch piece of cheesecloth and place thyme, peppercorns, allspice, bay leaf, and cinnamon stick in center. Tie into a bundle with kitchen twine; set aside.

Heat a large heavy skillet over medium-high heat; add 1 tablespoon rice oil. Cook ribs in batches in oil for 10 minutes or until dark brown on all sides, adding additional oil, if needed. Transfer ribs to a roasting pan. Drain all but 1 tablespoon of drippings from skillet.

Add carrots, celery, and onion to skillet. Cook over medium-high heat for 5 minutes or until golden brown, stirring constantly. Add bacon and cook for 1 minute, stirring constantly. Stir in tomato paste and cook for 1 minute. Spoon vegetable mixture over ribs and set aside.

Preheat oven to 300 degrees. Add wine to skillet. Bring to a boil, scraping up any browned bits. Simmer until mixture is reduced by three-fourths. Add spice bundle and pour wine reduction and veal stock over ribs. Cover tightly with aluminum foil.

Bake for 3 hours or until ribs are fork tender. Remove from oven and let cool in liquid. Remove ribs from liquid; cut away and discard excess fat and bones. Arrange ribs on a serving platter. Skim fat from braising liquid and bring to a boil over medium-high heat. Reduce heat and simmer for 20 to 25 minutes or until reduced by half. Remove spice bundle. Strain braising liquid through a mesh strainer, discarding vegetables. Pour braising liquid over ribs. Serve with Butternut Squash and Sautéed Greens.

BUTTERNUT SQUASH

1 (1½-pound) butternut squash, peeled and cut into bite-size pieces	¾ teaspoon kosher salt
1 tablespoon coconut oil	½ teaspoon harissa seasoning blend or chili garlic paste

Cook squash in boiling salted water to cover in a saucepan for 5 to 8 minutes or until tender; drain. Transfer to a blender and purée until smooth. Spoon into a bowl. Stir in coconut oil, salt, and harissa. Makes 4 servings.

SAUTÉED GREENS

8 ounces chard leaves	2 garlic cloves, thinly sliced
4 ounces mustard greens	1 tablespoon sherry vinegar
2 tablespoons extra-virgin olive oil	Kosher salt to taste
½ yellow onion, thinly sliced	

Trim stems from chard leaves and mustard greens. Cook in boiling salted water in a stockpot until wilted; drain. Rinse under cold running water. Drain and pat dry with paper towels.

Heat olive oil in a large skillet over low heat. Add onion and garlic; cook for 3 minutes or until light golden brown. Increase heat to medium and add greens to skillet. Cook for 5 to 6 minutes or until moisture evaporates and leaves are tender. Stir in vinegar and salt. Makes 4 servings.

Above: Before dinner, Chris hosted guests for a tasting of Lokoya's yet-to-be-released vintage of four unique mountain cabernet sauvignons. Opposite: Red Wine–Braised Short Ribs were served in bowls hand-thrown by a local potter.

Coffee-Crusted Rib-Eye Steak with Fig and Black Olive Pepperonata

Makes 4 servings

Consider cooking on an outdoor burner since searing the steak will produce a large amount of smoke.

1 (2½-pound) bone-in rib-eye steak	2 tablespoons butter, softened
1½ cups Coffee Rub	Fig and Black Olive Pepperonata
2 tablespoons vegetable oil	Microgreens

Remove steak from refrigerator and let stand at room temperature for 1 hour.

Preheat oven to 350 degrees. Heat a large cast-iron skillet over high heat. Sprinkle Coffee Rub evenly over all sides of steak. Add vegetable oil to hot skillet and immediately add steak. Cook for 6 minutes per side or until caramelized and crusted.

Transfer steak to a wire rack set in a roasting pan. Spread butter over steak. Bake for 25 minutes or until a meat thermometer inserted into thickest portion registers 110 to 120 degrees. Transfer to a cutting board and cover loosely with foil. Let rest for 10 minutes before carving (steak will continue to cook as it rests). Serve with Fig and Black Olive Pepperonata. Garnish with microgreens.

COFFEE RUB

1 tablespoon cumin seeds	1 tablespoon freshly ground black pepper
1 tablespoon fennel seeds	1 tablespoon ground white pepper
¼ cup ground coffee	1 tablespoon garlic powder
¼ cup kosher salt	2 teaspoons dried oregano
¼ cup smoked paprika	1 teaspoon cayenne pepper

Combine cumin seeds and fennel seeds in a small skillet over medium-high heat. Cook until seeds turn golden brown, shaking skillet occasionally. Transfer seeds to a bowl; cool.

Grind seeds in a spice grinder or crush in a mortar and pestle until finely ground. Combine the seed mixture, coffee, salt, paprika, black pepper, white pepper, garlic powder, oregano, and cayenne pepper in a small bowl and mix well. May store in an airtight container for up to 3 months. Makes 1 cup.

FIG AND BLACK OLIVE PEPPERONATA

2 tablespoons olive oil, divided	7 dried figs, quartered
½ cup red pearl onions, peeled and quartered, or ¼ cup chopped red onion	7 dry-cured black olives, pitted and chopped
4 small garlic cloves, thinly sliced	1½ teaspoons chopped fresh oregano
¼ cup roasted piquillo peppers or red bell pepper, diced	1 teaspoon pomegranate molasses
2 tablespoons toasted chopped walnuts	Kosher salt and freshly ground pepper to taste

Heat 1 tablespoon olive oil in a skillet over medium heat. Add pearl onions and garlic. Cook for 2 minutes or until tender and light golden brown. Stir in the remaining 1 tablespoon olive oil, peppers, walnuts, figs, olives, oregano, and molasses. Add salt and pepper. Makes 1 cup.

Opposite: Microgreens added color to the Coffee-Crusted Rib-Eye Steak. Right: Leather menu holders, cement-cast place card holders, cow horn napkin rings, embroidered napkins, and handblown glass added texture to the table.

An Abundance of Gratitude

One of the earliest wineries to be established in Napa Valley, Girard was founded in 1975 by Steve Girard and purchased by Pat Roney in 2000. Continuing the legacy of one of Napa's pioneering vintners is something Pat does not take lightly: his respect for the land and devotion to the craft of winemaking has kept Girard relevant, cutting edge, and authentically Napa.

When the Roney family and their close friends gather for Thanksgiving dinner each November, patriarch Pat Roney is the chef. Many men just cook the turkey, but Pat takes on the entire meal. For Pat, time in the kitchen is a stress reliever, giving him the opportunity to unplug and relax. He researches new recipes, pulls out old favorites, like his Country Pâté recipe, and thoroughly enjoys the entire process—from planning and shopping to cooking and feasting.

A spectacular Indian summer allowed the group to enjoy their afternoon repast outdoors. Pat's wife, Laura, and daughter-in-law, Brittany, set up several simple tables on the lawn. The vineyard, which showed a full display of fall colors, was a dramatic backdrop, so they kept the linens neutral and added natural centerpieces of persimmons, pears, olive branches, and fall leaves—all foraged on the property.

Supper for twenty began with warm butternut Soup de Courage, which Pat translates to "soup for the soul." The soup was topped with diced Granny Smith apples and fried sage. The family then enjoyed turkey with all the accompaniments, followed by an assortment of pies. Pat tasked his son, Sean, with selecting the wines for dinner. Sean chose Girard's Artistry saying, "The oak-influenced spice notes are similar to the spices Dad uses in cooking." Since Pat considers their four dogs to be family, he even baked treats so they could share in the feast.

"We gather together, open lots of great bottles of wine, and give thanks for each other and life's gifts," says Pat, who loves Thanksgiving because it is inclusive, family-oriented, and not commercial. This year, he was particularly grateful, as plans were moving forward to construct a magnificent new Girard winery in Calistoga.

Below: At Girard's tasting room in Yountville, visitors can enjoy their highly acclaimed wines in a relaxed rustic setting. Reservations are recommended for one-on-one tasting experiences. Opposite: Fall colors in the vineyard were the backdrop for Pat's Thanksgiving buffet.

Country Pâté with Beer and Fennel

Makes 20 servings

The Roney family eats this with cornichons or on a piece of crusty sourdough bread with mustard. Pat is happy to have a sip or two of beer while he's cooking.

4 ounces baguette or rustic Italian bread, torn	1½ pounds bulk sweet Italian turkey sausage, casings removed
2 tablespoons unsalted butter	1 cup imported beer, divided
1 large onion, chopped	½ pound ground veal
3 garlic cloves, minced	3 slices bacon, diced
4 green onions, sliced	1 teaspoon dried marjoram
¾ cup lightly packed chopped fresh parsley	¼ teaspoon dried oregano
¼ cup pistachios	¼ teaspoon dried sage
5 whole dried figs, halved	2–3 large eggs, lightly beaten
1 tablespoon fennel seeds	Salt and freshly ground pepper to taste

Place bread in a food processor and pulse until fine crumbs form (about 1¾ cups); set aside. Preheat oven to 325 degrees.

Melt butter in a large skillet over medium-high heat. Add onion, garlic, and green onions. Cook for 7 minutes or until soft and translucent. Transfer to a large mixing bowl and stir in parsley, pistachios, figs, and fennel seeds.

Add sausage to skillet and cook over medium-high heat for 2 to 3 minutes, stirring until crumbly. Stir in ½ cup beer and cook until sausage is no longer pink. Drain and stir into onion mixture. Add ground veal and ¼ cup beer to skillet; cook until veal is no longer pink, stirring until crumbly. Drain and stir into sausage mixture.

Cook bacon in skillet just until fat renders (do not cook until crisp). Stir into sausage mixture. Add reserved breadcrumbs, marjoram, oregano, sage, and remaining ¼ cup beer.

Add 2 eggs to pâté mixture and stir to make a moist, meatloaf-like mixture, adding an additional egg to bind mixture, if necessary. Stir in salt and pepper.

Pack mixture into a pâté terrine or 3x9-inch loaf pan, pressing firmly with hands or back of a spoon. Wrap tightly with aluminum foil. Place terrine in a roasting pan or 9x13-inch baking pan and fill with water to halfway up sides of terrine.

Bake for 1½ hours or until a meat thermometer inserted in center reads 165 degrees. Remove from oven and place on a wire rack. Weigh down pâté with canned goods or a wine bottle until cool. Chill for several hours or overnight. Run a knife around edges and invert onto a cutting board or platter. Pâté can be stored, tightly wrapped in plastic wrap and aluminum foil, in the refrigerator for 2 weeks or in the freezer for up to 2 months.

Above: Oven-roasted chestnuts on the buffet table. Persimmons, pears, mums, and fall leaves were used to decorate the table and buffet. Right: Baguettes and lavash crackers accompanied homemade pâté with dried figs.

"Every day we reflect on what we are thankful for. The love of family and friends, loyalty of customers, and beauty of Napa Valley are always top of mind." —PAT RONEY

Pat Roney

Pat's career in wine began as a sommelier at Chicago's Pump Room while in college. Upon graduation, Pat continued as the wine director and then went to work for The Seagram Wine Co. He returned to his native California to become president of Chateau St. Jean and then Kunde Estate. Leaving the industry for a brief stint, Pat served as CEO of gourmet food purveyor Dean & Deluca. He was lured back to wine in 2000, when the opportunity arose to purchase Girard.

Apple Pie

Makes 8 servings

- 2 pounds Jonathan, Honeycrisp, Granny Smith, Winesap, or other baking apples
- 2 tablespoons fresh lemon juice
- 2 tablespoons unsalted butter
- ½ cup sugar
- ½ teaspoon ground cinnamon
- ¼ teaspoon salt
- ¾ cup apple cider, divided
- 2 tablespoons cornstarch
- 1 tablespoon vanilla extract
- ¼ cup brandy
- Flaky Pie Dough

Peel, core, and slice apples; place in a large bowl. Add lemon juice, tossing to coat.

Melt butter in a large nonstick skillet over medium-high heat. Add apples and cook for 3 minutes, stirring occasionally. Stir sugar, cinnamon, and salt in a small bowl. Stir sugar mixture and ½ cup cider into apples. Reduce heat and cook for 5 to 7 minutes or until apples soften, stirring occasionally.

Combine cornstarch and remaining ¼ cup cider in a small cup. Stir into apple mixture and cook for 3 to 5 minutes or until thickened, stirring frequently. Stir in vanilla and brandy. Cool completely.

Preheat oven to 350 degrees. Roll 1 disk of pie dough into a 12-inch circle on a lightly floured surface. Fit dough into a 9-inch pie plate, leaving a ½-inch overhang. Roll the remaining disk into a 10-to 11-inch circle on a lightly floured surface. Cut into ¾-inch-wide strips.

Spoon apple filling into pie shell. Create a lattice top with dough strips. Fold bottom edge of crust over lattice edge, crimping edges to seal.

Place pie on a parchment- or foil-lined baking sheet. Bake for 50 to 60 minutes or until golden brown. Cool completely before slicing.

FLAKY PIE DOUGH

- 2¼ cups all-purpose flour
- ¼ teaspoon salt
- 1 cup unsalted butter, frozen
- ⅓ cup ice water

Combine flour and salt in a large bowl. Place a grate in bowl and coarsely grate frozen butter into flour. Toss mixture until butter is coated with flour. Sprinkle ⅓ cup water over butter mixture and stir gently just until blended. Add additional water, 1 tablespoon at a time, until dough holds together without crumbling (do not overwork dough). Divide and press into two flat disks; cover and chill for 1 hour. Makes 2 pie shells.

Including our Furry Friends

At many parties, the guest list includes a four-legged companion or two—or, at the Roney house, four. To make sure no one was left out, Pat baked treats to indulge his three beloved Borzois (Russian wolfhounds), Alexis, Boris, and Natasha, and his son's rescue pup, Clover, during the Thanksgiving feast. On the buffet were bone-shaped biscuits Pat made from pumpkin purée and bacon fat. "It's a great way to use leftover ingredients, and I think the dogs sense that they are being spoiled along with everyone else," says Pat. He often adds chopped parsley (a natural breath freshener), cheese, or peanut butter to his treats for the dogs. After the festivities, Pat sometimes makes doggie "trail mix" by dehydrating chunks of leftover meat and vegetables.

Opposite: Apple and pumpkin pies and a chocolate torte were served with vanilla bean ice cream or whipped cream. Left: Sean, Brittany, Pat and Laura Roney enjoy a glass of wine before the turkey is carved.

Brined and Roasted Turkey

Makes 10 to 12 servings

Several years ago, Pat discovered an Alton Brown episode on *Good Eats* titled "Romancing the Bird." Alton's mission of breaking the dry turkey curse aligned with Pat's goal for a juicy turkey. Brining and roasting a turkey using Alton's method is now a Thanksgiving tradition.

1 (14- to 16-pound) turkey	1 red apple, sliced
1 gallon (16 cups) vegetable stock or broth	½ onion, sliced
1 cup kosher salt	1 cinnamon stick
½ cup firmly packed light brown sugar	1 cup water
1 tablespoon whole black peppercorns	4 sprigs of fresh rosemary
1½ teaspoons whole allspice	6 sage leaves
1½ teaspoons chopped candied ginger	Canola oil
1 gallon (16 cups) ice water	

Thaw turkey, if frozen, for 2 to 3 days in a refrigerator or ice-filled cooler. Remove neck, tail, and giblets and discard or save for another use.

Combine vegetable stock, salt, brown sugar, peppercorns, allspice, and ginger in a large stockpot over medium-high heat. Bring to a boil. Cook until salt and sugar dissolve, stirring occasionally. Cool to room temperature; refrigerate.

Combine brine with 1 gallon ice water in a 5-gallon bucket or cooler. Rinse turkey inside and out. Lower turkey, breast side down, into brine, weighing down, if necessary, to submerge entire bird. Cover and chill for 8 to 16 hours, turning once.

Preheat oven to 500 degrees with rack on lowest level. Lift turkey from brine, rinse, and pat dry. Place turkey on a wire rack in a large roasting pan.

Combine apple, onion, cinnamon stick, and 1 cup water in a glass bowl. Microwave on High for 5 minutes. Spoon apple mixture, rosemary, and sage into turkey cavity. Tuck wings underneath and coat skin generously with canola oil.

Roast turkey for 30 minutes. Reduce oven temperature to 350 degrees. Roast for 1½ to 2 hours or until a meat thermometer inserted through thickest part of breast registers 161 degrees (turkey will continue to cook). Transfer to a platter and cover with foil. Let rest for 15 minutes before carving.

Menu

Country Pâté with Beer and Fennel
Salmon Pâté
Soup de Courage
Brined and Roasted Turkey
Focaccia Stuffing
Mashed Potatoes
Candied Yams
Roasted Root Vegetables
Green Salad
Cranberry Relish
Turkey Gravy
Pumpkin Pie
Apple Pie
All-American Chocolate Torte

Russian River Chardonnay
Mixed Blacks Red Wine
Artistry Cabernet Sauvignon

Opposite: The Thanksgiving meal featured many flavors. Pat served Girard's flagship wine, Artistry,

a classic red bordeaux blend with notes of red, black, and blue fruits and oak-influenced spice

nuances, because it offers something delicious to pair with this most American of feasts. Above: Pat

brines his turkey for sixteen hours to season it from the inside out and keep it moist and juicy.

Family Traditions

Opposite: Guests gathered for a harvest dinner in "Jack and Jamie's Grove," surrounded by ancient olive trees and Diamond Mountain Cabernet vines. Below: The estate's 1880s Victorian has been the Davies family home since 1965. At their historic Calistoga property, visitors can taste sparkling and still wines, learn about the *méthode traditionnelle* process, and tour the historic caves.

The Diamond Mountain estate, founded in 1862 by Jacob Schram, was purchased by Jack and Jamie Davies in 1965. Pioneers in Napa Valley, the Davies painstakingly restored the property and set out to produce sparkling wine under the Schramsberg label. They quickly made a name for themselves when their fifth vintage was served at the "Toast to Peace" State Dinner in Beijing, China, with President Richard Nixon and Premier Chou En-lai.

Since then, the Davies family has established many traditions around harvest and the holidays. Jack and Jamie's youngest son, Hugh—now president of the winery—and his wife, Monique, carry on these customs to engage their own three sons in the family business. "We share my parents' passions," says Hugh, "and want to preserve their legacy."

During harvest, Hugh and Monique gathered colleagues and friends to bless the grapes and show their gratitude for another year's abundant crop—a practice Jamie had started with the very first vintage. Monique set a long table in the olive tree lane known as "Jack and Jamie's Grove." Guests brought dishes for the family-style meal. Friend Bert Casten roasted a whole lamb over an open fire. It was a perfect match with the Davies Vineyards red wines, particularly the J. Davies Estate "Jamie."

To ring in the Christmas season, the family and close friends enjoyed dinner in the formal dining room of their Victorian house. "The Christmas holiday is sacred to us," explains Monique. "We want our boys to share the same magical experiences Hugh did as a boy growing up in this house." The meal included J. Schram Tête de Cuvée and Black River Caviar because, as Monique says, "bubbles and caviar are the quintessential holiday extravagance, and Jamie loved caviar." Heirloom gold-rimmed porcelain plates, silver flatware, silver candelabra, and cut crystal gave the table a timeless feel.

History, family, rituals, and the environment play a big role in the Davies's life and have a profound influence on how Hugh and Monique raise their boys—just like Jack and Jamie brought up their three sons four decades earlier.

Clockwise from top left: J. Davies "Jamie" Cabernet Sauvignon pays homage to Hugh's mother. A lamb cooked over an open fire was served family-style. Gerbera daisies added brilliance to fall centerpieces. A rosemary broom was used to baste lamb with olive oil, red wine, beer, and herbs.

The Davies Family

Born the year his parents purchased Schramsberg, Hugh Davies has been immersed in the wine business his entire life. Hugh earned a master's degree in enology from UC Davis, honing his skills in France and Australia and at other California wineries before joining Schramsberg's winemaking team. Hugh was named president in 2005. He and his wife, Monique, are raising their sons, Emrys, Nelson, and Hugh, Jr., to carry the mantle forward.

"With the support of family and friends, we are hopeful that history will repeat itself and that the next generation will carry the family legacy into the future." —MONIQUE DAVIES

Clockwise from right: Heirloom china added elegance to the table. The Davies family and friends gathered for hors d'oeuvres and a bit of monkey business in the living room. The dining room was set for a formal holiday dinner.

Top left: In the centerpiece, glass bubbles represented the sparkling wine. Above: Garlands of bay leaves, evergreen branches, pomegranates, and hydrangeas framed the living room windows.

Bacon and Eggs

Makes 8 servings

1 pound pork belly or center-cut slab bacon	1 teaspoon whole black peppercorns
¼ white onion, diced	1 bay leaf
6 cups vegetable stock or broth	1 cup dry white vermouth
1 head cauliflower, cut into small florets	1 (125 gram) container Black River Oscietra caviar, divided
4 cups heavy whipping cream	1 heaping teaspoon thinly sliced chives
3 tablespoons unsalted butter	Fresh chive pieces
Salt and ground white pepper to taste	
1 shallot, minced	

Preheat oven to 300 degrees. Remove skin from pork belly, leaving ¼ inch of fat on meat and reserving skin. Combine pork, onion, and vegetable stock in a Dutch oven. Bake, covered, for 1½ to 2 hours or until very tender when pierced with a fork. Remove from oven and cool pork in liquid until at room temperature.

Meanwhile, combine cauliflower, cream, butter, and salt in a large saucepan over medium-high heat. Bring to a boil. Reduce heat and simmer for 10 to 14 minutes or until florets are tender and cream mixture is reduced by one-fourth (do not scorch). Transfer cauliflower to a blender with a slotted spoon, reserving cream mixture. Blend at medium speed, slowly adding enough cream mixture (about 2 tablespoons) to cauliflower until it reaches the consistency of pudding. Season with salt and white pepper. Set aside.

Slice or chop a fourth of the reserved pork belly skin, discarding remaining skin. Place in a small saucepan or skillet over medium-low heat. Cook for 10 to 15 minutes, stirring frequently. Add shallot, peppercorns, and bay leaf to drippings. Increase heat to medium-high. Cook for 2 minutes or until shallots are translucent, stirring frequently. Stir in vermouth. Bring mixture to a boil. Reduce heat and simmer for 6 to 8 minutes or until reduced by three-fourths. Stir in reserved cream mixture; simmer for 10 minutes or until thickened. Strain cream sauce through a mesh strainer. Set aside.

Remove pork from braising liquid and cut into 8 equal portions. Arrange on a baking sheet. Increase oven temperature to 350 degrees. Bake for 4 to 5 minutes or until heated through.

Place serving plates in oven until warm. Reheat cream sauce over low heat until warm. Fold in 2 tablespoons caviar and sliced chives. Spoon 2 to 3 tablespoons of cauliflower purée onto center of each plate. Create a well with the back of a large spoon, using a circular motion to spread purée. Spoon about 1 or 2 tablespoons cream sauce onto purée and top with pork belly. Top each evenly with the remaining caviar and garnish with a piece of fresh chive.

Note: The remaining cauliflower purée and cream sauce can be covered and refrigerated for up to 3 days.

Top: Monique adjusts son Nelson's bow tie. Above: A library vintage of J. Schram was served with Black River Caviar on homemade potato chips. Right: Chef Walter Manzke's playful pork belly and caviar dish that he calls "Bacon and Eggs" is topped with Black River Caviar.

Potato and Leek Soup

Makes 4 servings

Chef Walter Manzke of Los Angeles's renowned République joined the Davies to create some incredible dishes using friend Graham Gaspard's Black River Caviar. They were a superb pairing with the sparkling wines.

9 leeks, divided
4 cups vegetable broth
1 cup heavy whipping cream
3 tablespoons unsalted butter
Salt to taste

3 large Yukon gold potatoes, peeled and cubed
½ teaspoon white pepper
1 (125 gram) container Black River Oscietra caviar

Remove root and green tops of leeks and rinse leeks under running water. Slice 5 leeks ⅛ inch thick and soak in cold water to remove excess grit; drain.

Combine vegetable broth and cream in a medium saucepan over medium heat and bring to a simmer. Keep warm.

Melt butter in a large saucepan over medium heat. Add sliced leeks and salt. Cook for 7 to 10 minutes or until leeks are translucent, stirring frequently. Add potatoes and cook for 2 minutes, stirring frequently. Stir in broth mixture. Cook over medium heat for 16 to 18 minutes or until potatoes and leeks are tender, stirring frequently.

Purée with an immersion blender or process in batches in a blender until smooth. Add white pepper and salt.

For cold soup, pour soup into a large bowl set inside a bowl of ice water. Stir until cool. Cover and chill until ready to serve. For warm soup, pour soup back into saucepan and keep warm over low heat.

Steam or boil the remaining 4 whole leeks for 6 to 8 minutes or until tender. Plunge in ice water to cool; drain and pat dry with paper towels. Slice leeks ½ inch thick.

To serve cold soup, place 8 to 10 leek slices in each chilled bowl. Top each with 1 ounce of caviar. Pour chilled soup around leeks, leaving tops of leeks exposed. To serve hot soup, preheat oven to 300 degrees. Place 8 to 10 leek slices in each ovenproof bowl. Cover with plastic wrap and place on a baking sheet. Bake for 3 to 4 minutes or until bowls are hot and filled with steam. Remove from oven and let stand for 5 minutes. Remove plastic wrap and top each with 1 ounce of caviar. Pour warm soup around leeks.

Top: A generous serving of Black River Caviar topped the Potato and Leek Soup. Above: Chocolates from Flourish Chocolate, a local chocolatier, were intended as gifts for the guests until the boys discovered them.

Pay Us a Visit

A though small in size, Napa Valley is massive in reputation. Considered one of the most notable wine growing regions in the world, Napa is just thirty miles long and a few miles wide, with 45,000 acres of vineyards planted.

Each of the hosts included in *Napa Valley Entertaining* has extended an open invitation to come and visit. While they represent a small handful of the valley's more than 500 wineries, they capture the diversity that makes touring in Napa Valley so compelling. To see them all provides an impressive education on the valley's range of terroir—from the cool breezes in Carneros and the dust of Rutherford to the mountain slopes of the Vaca and Mayacama.

1. Ceja Vineyards
2. The Aviary at Ackerman Heritage House
3. Bounty Hunter Rare Wine & Spirits
4. Palmaz Vineyards
5. Whetstone Wine Cellars
6. Trefethen Family Vineyards
7. Regusci Ranch
8. Atelier Fine Foods
9. Girard Winery
10. Barbara Colvin & Co.
11. Gemstone Vineyard
12. Silver Oak Cellars
13. B Cellars
14. Gargiulo Vineyards
15. Alpha Omega
16. BRAND Napa Valley
17. Chappellet Vineyard
18. Raymond Vineyards
19. Sorensen Catering
20. Davies Vineyards
21. Clif Family Winery
22. Meadowood Napa Valley
23. Lokoya
24. Schramsberg Vineyards
25. CONSTANT Diamond Mountain Vineyard
26. Frank Family Vineyards
27. Davis Estates
28. Clark-Claudon Vineyards
29. Phifer Pavitt Wine

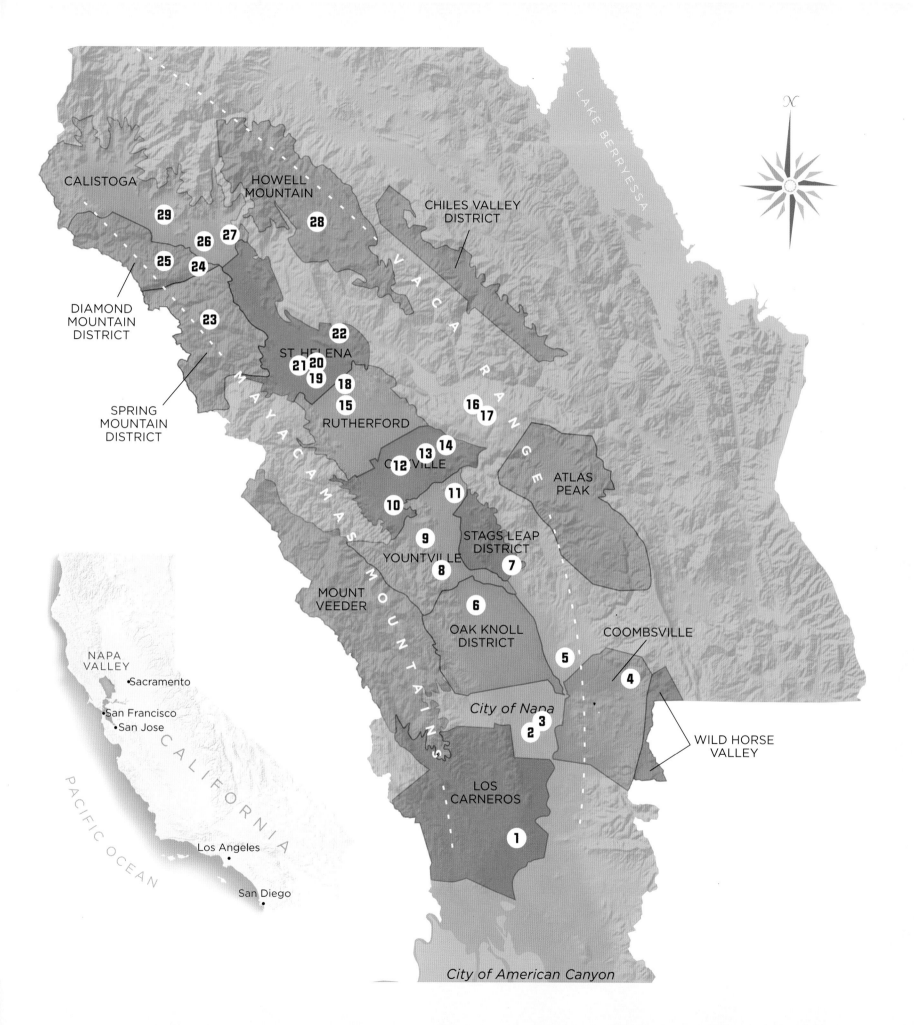

CALISTOGA

HOWELL
MOUNTAIN

CHILES VALLEY
DISTRICT

29

28

26 27

25

24

DIAMOND
MOUNTAIN
DISTRICT

23

22

ST. HELENA

21 20

19

18

SPRING
MOUNTAIN
DISTRICT

15

RUTHERFORD

16

17

ATLAS
PEAK

14

13

12 OAKVILLE

11

10

STAGS LEAP
DISTRICT

9

YOUNTVILLE

7

8

MOUNT
VEEDER

6

OAK KNOLL
DISTRICT

COOMBSVILLE

5

4

City of Napa

2 3

WILD HORSE
VALLEY

LOS
CARNEROS

1

City of American Canyon

NAPA
VALLEY

•Sacramento

•San Francisco

•San Jose

CALIFORNIA

PACIFIC OCEAN

•Los Angeles

•San Diego

LAKE BERRYESSA

VACA RANGE

MAYACAMAS MOUNTAINS

Hosts

Ackerman Family Vineyards
2101 Kirkland Road
Napa, CA 94558
(855) 238-9463
ackermanfamilyvineyards.com

Alpha Omega
1155 Mee Lane
St. Helena, CA 94574
Rutherford AVA
(707) 963-9999
aowinery.com

Auction Napa Valley
Napa Valley Vintners
1475 Library Lane
St. Helena, CA 94574
(707) 963-3388
auctionnapavalley.org

B Cellars
703 Oakville Cross Road
Oakville, CA 94562
(707) 709-8787
bcellars.com

Bounty Hunter Rare Wine & Spirits
975 First Street
Napa, CA 94559
(800) 943-9463
bountyhunterwine.com

BRAND Napa Valley
90 Long Ranch Road
St. Helena, CA 94574
(707) 963-1199
brandnapavalley.com

Ceja Vineyards
1016 Las Amigas Road
Napa, CA 94559
(707) 255-3954
cejavineyards.com

Chappellet Vineyard
Pritchard Hill
St. Helena, CA 94574
(707) 286-4219
chappellet.com

Clark-Claudon Vineyards
(707) 965-9393
clarkclaudon.com

Clif Family Winery Velo Vino
709 Main Street
St. Helena, CA 94574
(707) 968-0625
cliffamilywinery.com

Barbara Colvin & Co.
(707) 948-9800
bcolvinco.com

CONSTANT Diamond Mountain Vineyard
2121 Diamond Mountain Road
Calistoga, CA 94515
(707) 942-0707
constantwine.com

Davis Estates
4060 Silverado Trail N,
Calistoga, CA 94515
(707) 942-0700
davisestates.com

davies vineyards
1210 Grayson Avenue
St. Helena, CA 94574
(707) 963-5555
DaviesVineyards.com

Frank Family Vineyards
1091 Larkmead Lane
Calistoga, CA 94515
(707) 942-0859
frankfamilyvineyards.com

Gargiulo Vineyards
575 Oakville Crossroad
Napa, CA 94558
(707) 944-2770
gargiulovineyards.com

Gemstone Vineyard
PO Box 3477
Yountville, CA 94599
(707) 944-0944
gemstonevineyard.com

Girard Napa Valley
6795 Washington Street
Yountville, CA 94599
(707) 921-2795
girardwinery.com

Lokoya
3787 Spring Mountain Road
St. Helena, CA 94574
(707) 948-1968
lokoya.com

Meadowood Napa Valley
900 Meadowood Lane
St. Helena, CA 94574
(707) 531-4788
meadowood.com

Palmaz Vineyards
4029 Hagen Road
Napa, CA 94558
(707) 226-5587
palmazvineyards.com

Phifer Pavitt Wine
4660 Silverado Trail
Calistoga, CA 94515
(707) 942-4787
phiferpavittwine.com

Raymond Vineyards
849 Zinfandel Lane
St. Helena, CA 94574
(707) 963-3141
raymondvineyards.com

Regusci Ranch Winery
5584 Silverado Trail
Napa, CA 94558
(707) 254-0403
regusciwinery.com

Schramsberg Vineyards
1400 Schramsberg Road
Calistoga CA 94515
(707) 942-4558
schramsberg.com

Silver Oak Cellars
915 Oakville Crossroad
Oakville, CA 94562
(707) 942-7022
silveroak.com

Sorensen Catering
677 St. Helena Highway
St. Helena, CA 94574
(707) 967-9022
sorensencatering.com

Trefethen Family Vineyards
1160 Oak Knoll Avenue West
Napa, CA 94558
(866) 895-7696
trefethen.com

Whetstone Wine Cellars
1075 Atlas Peak Road
Napa, CA 94558
(707) 254-0600
whetstonewinecellars.com

Resources

The Aviary at Ackerman Heritage House
- Tasting salon
608 Randolph Street
Napa, CA 94559
(855) 238-9463
ackermanheritagehouse.com

Alpha Omega
Big Poppa smokers
- BBQ sauce, rubs, and smokers
53973 Polk Street
Coachella, CA 92236
(877) 828-0727
bigpoppasmokers.com

L.A. Hearn Company
- King City Pink beans
512 Metz Road
King City, CA 93930
(831) 385-5441
hearneco.com

ThermoWorks
- Thermapen meat thermometer
(800) 393-6434
thermoworks.com

Auction Napa Valley
Mustard's Grill
- Chef Cindy Pawlcyn restaurant
7399 St. Helena Highway
Napa, CA 94558
(707) 944-2424
mustardsgrill.com

Quince
- Chef Michael Tusk restaurant
470 Pacific Avenue
San Francisco, CA 94133
(415) 775-8500
quincerestaurant.com

B Cellars
Rion Designs
- Floral and event design
899 Dowdell Lane
St. Helena, CA 94574
(707) 416-2921
riondesigns.com

Bounty Hunter Rare Wine & Spirits
Dione Carston
Fine Hoarding
- Table design
(707) 738-6969

BRAND Napa Valley
A X Events
- Event design
(707) 333-1122
axevent.com

La Saison
- Catering
748 California Blvd
Napa, CA 94559
(707) 637-3722
lasaison.net

Briana Marie Photography
(707) 738-8224
brianamariephotography.com

Chappellet Vineyard
NBC Pottery
- Hand thrown ceramics
380 Eastern Avenue
Angwin, CA 94508
(707) 965-1007

Clark-Claudon Vineyards
NBC Pottery
- Hand thrown ceramics
380 Eastern Avenue
Angwin, CA 94508
(707) 965-1007

Clif Family Winery
Hive Napa
- Event design
HiveNapaCa.com

Clif Family Bruschetteria
- Restaurant on wheels
(707)301-7188
cliffamily.com/visit-us/#bruschetteria-food-truck

Davis Estates
Rion Designs
- Floral and event design
899 Dowdell Lane
St. Helena, CA 94574
(707) 416-2921
riondesigns.com

Frank Family
Rion Designs
Floral and event design
899 Dowdell Lane
St. Helena, CA 94574
(707) 416-2921
riondesigns.com

Tre Posti
Chef Nash Cognetti
- Catering
641 Main Street
St. Helena, CA 94574
(707) 963-7600
treposti.com

Gemstone Vineyard
Centerpiece Floral & Home
- Floral design
1422 Main Street
St. Helena, CA 94574
(707) 963-5700
centerpiecenapavalley.com

Lokoya
Mahon Ceramics
- Dinner plates
7111 Dry Creek Rd,
Napa, CA 94558
(707) 944-8842
lynnmahon.com

Meadowood Napa Valley
Estate Events by Meadowood
- Catering and Event design
900 Meadowood Lane
St. Helena, CA 94574
(707) 531-4788
meadowood.com

Phifer Pavitt Wine
ROQUE Events
- Event planning
(707) 628-9998
Roqueevents.com

Laura Lambrix Designs
- Graphic Design
(530) 680-1359
lauralambrixdesigns.com

Mae Flowers
- Florist
(707) 363-8439
maeflowerssonoma.com

One True Love Vintage Rentals
- Carpet and accessory rentals
417 Allan Street
Daly City, CA 94014
(415) 741-5884
onetruevintage.com

The Model Bakery
- Muffins and pastries
1357 Main Street
St. Helena, CA 94574
(707) 963-1892
themodelbakery.com

Panevino Food for Wine
- Cheese, charcuterie and breadsticks
1080 Fulton Lane #C
St. Helena, CA 94574
(707) 963-2786
panevino-napavalley.mybigcommerce.com

Encore Events Rentals
- Party rentals
434 Payran Street, Suite B
Petaluma, CA 94954
(707) 763-3322
encoreeventsrentals.com

La Tavola Fine Linens
- Linen rentals
2655 Napa Valley Corporate Drive
Napa, CA 94558
(707) 257-3358
latavolalinen.com

Raymond Vineyards
Atelier Fine Foods
- Cheese, charcuterie
6505 Washington Street
Yountville, CA 94599
(707) 934-8237
jcbcollection.com/location/atelier-by-jcb-yountville

JCB Collection
- Crystal, china & jewelry
6505 Washington Street
Yountville, CA 94599
(707) 934-8237
jcbcollection.com

Schramsberg Vineyards
Black River Caviar USA
- Caviar
(970) 418-0114
blackrivercaviar.com

FLOURISH Chocolate
- Artisan chocolates
flourishchocolate.com
(707) 942-9494

Silver Oak Cellars
Rion Designs
- Event and floral design
899 Dowdell Lane
St. Helena, CA 94574
(707) 416-2921
riondesigns.com

Sorensen Catering
Stag's Leap Wine Cellars
- Event location
5766 Silverado Trail
Napa, CA 94558
(707) 261-6410
cask23.com

Whetstone Wine Cellars
SMOKE Open Fire Napa
- Catering
2766 Old Sonoma Road
Napa, CA 94558
(707) 927-5070
smokeopenfire.com

Prune & Paper
Alli van Zyl
- Menu design
(510) 304-7902
www.pruneandpaper.com

Melody Raye Flowers and Design
Melody Mahoney
- Floral design
(415) 999-2215
www.melodyraye.com

Index

Historic Hospitality Books

Napa Valley Entertaining was published by Historic Hospitality Books in collaboration with Blakesley Chappellet. Historic Hospitality Books is an imprint of Southwestern Publishing Group, Inc., 2451 Atrium Way, Nashville, Tennessee 37214. Southwestern Publishing Group is a wholly owned subsidiary of Southwestern/Great American, Inc., Nashville, Tennessee.

Christopher G. Capen, President, Southwestern Publishing Group, Inc.
Sheila Thomas, Publisher, Historic Hospitality Books
Vicky Shea, Cover and Layout Designer
Betsy Holt, Editor
Kristin Connelly, Managing Editor
Julia Rutland, Recipe Tester/Editor
Linda Brock, Proofreader
www.swpublishinggroup.com | 800-358-0560

ISBN: 978-0-87197-644-4
Library of Congress Control Number: 2017933415
Printed in China
10 9 8 7 6 5 4 3 2 1

Cover and interior photographs © Briana Marie Photography

Additional photography by:
136 - Steven Rothfeld Photography
153 - Sylvain Gentile Photography
160, 166 - Molly Chappellet, Photographer
165 - Julia Crane, Photographer
172 - Napa Valley Register
176 - Brent Broza Photography
188 - Adrian Gregorutti, Photographer
191 - Sara Sanger, Photographer
197 - Gustavo Fernández Photography
204 - Andy Katz Photography
218 - Timm Eubanks Photography